PROPHESY

TORN CURTAIN PUBLISHING
Auckland, New Zealand
www.torncurtainpublishing.com

ISBN Softcover 978-1-991299-61-1
ISBN ePub 978-1-991299-62-8

Typeset in Neue Haas Grotesk, Minion Pro, Connoisseurs

Cataloging in Publishing Data
 Title: Prophesy
 Author: Jenny Gilpin
 Subjects: Prophecy, Christian living, devotional, inspirational, personal growth, spiritual growth, prophetic ministry, Christian leadership, daily devotions

A copy of this title is held at the National Library of New Zealand.

PROPHESY

UNLOCKING YOUR NEW SEASON OF BREAKTHROUGH

84 DECLARATIONS
UNPACKED
FROM GOD'S WORD TO YOU

JENNY GILPIN

I have known Pastor Jenny since she was teenage girl hungrily seeking after God at youth camps where I spoke. That passion and deep hunger for God has never abated. Now as a powerful and significant woman of God her compassion for people and tenacious pressing into God is more intense than ever. This book will inspire and take you to a deeper place in Your walk with Jesus.

—**Tim Hall**
Global Evangelist

One of the greatest gifts we have been given is the gift of prophesy- the awesome ability to speak from Gods' perspective, to declare 'Yes and Amen', and to see manifest the perfect will and heart of God in our lives! Thank you Jenny for reminding us that God's promises, when faith- fully declared, are powerful and transformational. This book will shift destinies and change lives.

—**Leanne Matthesius**
Senior Pastor of Awaken Church, San Diego

The power of prophecy cannot be underestimated. just as God created the universe through speaking, so we too create our worlds with our words. And when they are the words of God Himself, nothing is impossible. Thanks Jenny for putting together such an important of creative declarations. Those who take from this book what's been declared and prophesied will transform their world.

—**Phil Pringle**
President, C3 Global

Dedicated to Pastor David Cartledge, whose prophetic words both framed and empowered my future.

The prophetic word is in you. It's like a seed that will soon grow into the tallest of trees. It's like 'a cloud the size of a man's hand' that will soon create a flood that moves everything out of its path. God's word contains enough power to do all that it promises, yet is only released as we dare to prophesy it into being. Prophesying is what has caused walls to fall, armies to rise, wombs to open and new seasons to begin.

Let this book lead you into your greatest season ever,

For you,

Jenny Gilpin

CONTENTS

SECTION ONE
GOD IS MINDFUL

'The word of the Lord came to me, saying, "Before I formed you in the womb I knew you, before you were born I set you apart; I appointed you as a prophet to the nations."'

JEREMIAH 1:4-5

He knew you before you were born. He had you on His heart and mind when Isaiah wrote, 'He was bruised for our transgressions' (Isaiah 53:5). He knew you before the world was created, 'He chose us in Him before the creation of the world . . . ' (Ephesians 1:4). For as long as God has been God, you have been on His heart and in His thoughts. His thoughts to you are more than the number of grains of sand in all the beaches in the world. And He knows how many hairs are on your head. Great and small, significant and insignificant—He is mindful.

DECLARATION ONE

I AM A CHILD OF THE INVISIBLE

*Then Jesus got into the boat and started across the lake with His
disciples. Suddenly, a fierce storm struck the lake, with waves
breaking into the boat. But Jesus was sleeping. The disciples went
and woke Him up, shouting, "Lord, save us! We are going to
drown." Jesus responded, "Why are you afraid? You have so little
faith." Then He got up and rebuked the wind and the waves, and
suddenly there was a great calm.*
MATTHEW 8:23 -26

Faith is a confidence that what is unseen is ours. The realities of
our future are thirsty for the faith of our present. In Matthew 8, Jesus
is teaching us to stay in faith, whilst everyone else is flailing around.
God is teaching us to be confident in the storm and supreme in our rest,
and to be confident in faith that the future is greater than the moment.

There is an invincible summer arising within you, a faith that propels
you forward through thick and thin—a trust, a hope and an expectation
that can only be forged in the furnace of fear.

Every part of your today is preparation for your tomorrow.

*He kept right on going because he kept his eyes
on the one who is invisible.*
HEBREWS 11:27

God has amazing plans for each and every one of our lives. God has extreme plans for His church. All future greatness starts with a tremendous thirst, a thirst for more, a relentless quest for greater things. Your future demands something of you. It demands a quest in you to be a child of the invisible. The miracles of the future demand you to be seeing stuff in your spirit that cannot now be seen with the natural eye.

What do you see? What you see around you today in all of the testimonies of lives saved and transformed did not come from the natural realm. They existed in God's heart and in the spirits of people who chose to see the impossible. They chose to walk by faith and not by sight.

Today exists because a body of people chose to be tent dwellers—people who lived for the eternal and chose not to settle in the comfort of what they thought they could handle. Our future relies on us taking this opportunity to be those people again, to see beyond the visible and into the power of the God of the invisible.

The eye of faith is an inner TV screen that is playing unseen footage even before it is written. I am already watching an unwritten screenplay of my family, an unseen screenplay of the church, an unseen screenplay of an unprecedented move of God and unseen screenplays of miraculous healings and deliverances.

What are you already watching before you see it? What are you viewing on the screen of your heart?

Father,
Open the eyes of my heart to see your eternal Kingdom and your eternal truths standing over me. Let faith arise in my heart—the type of faith that is not daunted by the size of the wave or the weight of the problem. I thank you that the future is mine. Today, I identify as one who lives by faith, walks in faith and steps out in faith until I see your Kingdom come and your will be done.
In Jesus' name, Amen.

DECLARATION TWO

HE WILL CARRY ME THROUGH

*Let us not become weary in doing good, for at the proper
time we will reap a harvest if we do not give up.*
GALATIANS 6:9

Do you feel weary? This scripture is not a command to not be weary, but an inspiration that you're closer to your answer than ever before. it's there because our Father knows the condition of our human hearts and knows that there are times when the sheer weight of it all is too much.

Often, it is not actually what we carry that overwhelms us, but the perception of our own inability to carry that weight. It comes from an inability to see into the unseen and see that God is holding all of the threads of our lives together. He is actually carrying us through.

Life often brings seasons when the weight of it all seems unbearable. If you are in that season today, God the Holy Spirit is going to touch your life so you can see His majesty and capability to carry you, help you and see you through to harvest. We should also be aware that the enemy of our souls uses 'overwhelming' to discourage us and knock us off course. We all have moments of overwhelming tiredness, overwhelming discouragement, overwhelming anger and the overwhelming

desire to quit, when the cost just seems too great.

Be self controlled and alert. Your enemy the devil prowls around
like a roaring lion looking for someone to devour.
Resist him, standing firm in the faith ...
1 PETER 5:8-9

Sometimes it's a wave of emotion we are feeling, sometimes it's more than that. Today, God is causing you to look again and to turn your attention to His future for you; to be one who decides to live a life of ruling both your soul and your emotions. God will come through. He's promised it. It's time to rest in that promise.

Father,
Help me to realise that with you I am actually a lot stronger than I think. I am full of faith and full of resolve. The ups and downs of life have created a hardened veteran within me that doesn't fall under the side-swipes of the enemy.
I am not a quitter! As long as there is one more person to touch, my life will remain unwearied, unsullied and full of purpose.
I am convinced that just at the right time, a harvest will appear because my God has promised it.
In Jesus' name, Amen.

DECLARATION THREE

HE IS THE GUARDIAN OF MY DESTINY

*As for God, His way is perfect. The Lord's word is flawless; He
shields all who take refuge in Him.*
PSALM 18:30

God's dream for humanity outweighs the transient and flawed promises
of men.

God's dream for your life is so huge that He sacrificed His sinless,
one and only Son just for you, in order that you again could have a
friendship and walk with Him—that you could walk with God again
in the cool of the day and know the beauty of His presence and the
succour of His plan.

God has a dream for your life.

He is not satisfied with the oppression and the sin that entangles us.
He has fought for you and continues to fight and intercede for your life.

*In all their distress He too was distressed, and the angel of His
presence saved them. In His love and mercy He redeemed them;
He lifted them up and carried them all the days of old.*
ISAIAH 63:9

He feels for you, fights for you and has prepared a way for you. He
is, in a sense, the guardian of your destiny and the bodyguard of your
dream. As His followers, we are called to be more like Jesus, and as

prophetic beings, it's this guardianship that He invites you into. You too are called to be a bodyguard and a part of God's dream for humanity.

Joseph, the husband of Mary, became the very first guardian of God's dream for humanity. He was the first and the best example of bodyguarding.

> *When Joseph woke up, he did what the angel of The Lord*
> *had commanded him and took Mary home as his wife.*
> *But he had no union with her until she gave birth to a son.*
> *And he gave him the name Jesus.*
> **MATTHEW 1:24-25**

Joseph was put in an impossible position but something within him understood in a small way the magnitude of that position. He became the guardian of the sole source of eternity for the soul of humanity. His agenda was completely submitted to the cause of He whom he worshipped. Joseph housed the heartbeat of God through a listening ear.

Joseph's name is still known today but in his own lifetime his importance was not immediately obvious. He said little, but he moved in miracles—he acted prophetically.

God wants to restore to you today a sense of the magnitude of that which He has placed within you.

You may never be famous but your significance is eternal.

Father,
Reawaken within me a sense of your calling and a deep sense of the significance you have placed upon my life. I take up your invitation to become a bodyguard of the dream and purposes of God in my generation and in the generations to come. Give me the strength to protect and the open ear to hear all that the Spirit of God is whispering for me to do. In Jesus' name, Amen.

DECLARATION FOUR

I HAVE A HEAVENLY CONFIDENCE

As the Philistine moved closer to attack him, David ran quickly toward the battle line to meet him. Reaching into his bag and taking out a stone, he slung it and struck the Philistine on the forehead.

1 SAMUEL 17:48-49

Today many of you are facing the giant of intimidation. You are facing the voice that says you have nothing at all to say, but the God of your life speaks again into your spirit and says, 'Rise up, be the voice and don't back down. This is your moment to be all that I have called you to be.'

In David's story, a whole generation were intimidated into silence by a giant that presented himself bigger than their own ability to overcome.

Things come and try to intimidate us. They're not little annoyances like an itch or an ache—they are designed to be opponents to our destiny. Sometimes, it's like there is a roaring Goliath-sized voice in our heads telling us to sit down, to submit to smallness and remain silent in opposition. This voice seeks to deny our peace, our confidence, our destiny and our inheritance.

So often, the Goliaths that we face are attacks on our minds. Intimidation comes to threaten the size of God in your mind. God is greater than anything we face, yet intimidation tells you that your emotional, financial or personal situation is so big and so insurmountable that you need to sit down and be quiet in response to them.

We need to prophesy to that Goliath, and see the roar for what it really is—a sound that's designed to silence us. As we open our mouths, as we make our own sound, we rob that intimidation of its power over us.

The giants that have faced you are actually a complimentary statement that a great future lies ahead. Today, the silenced will find their voice, find their fight, and will see again the size of their God. This will turn out to be your finest hour and your greatest breakthrough.

Father,
I choose to believe that the God inside of me is bigger, stronger and more powerful than any other force seeking to silence or stop me. I prophesy my victory and my faith. I see my future and commit to taking the right steps to see it all come to pass.
In Jesus' name, Amen.

DECLARATION FIVE

I WILL NOT FEAR

For God has not given us a spirit of fear, but of power
and of love and of a sound mind.
2 TIMOTHY 1:7

How often do we feel fearful? Fear challenges your trust in God's faithfulness and tries to strangle the prophetic voice that is welling up on the inside of us. Fear speaks to us and threatens us with the wrong outcome.

Fear tells us to sit down, and tells us that we have nothing to say.

Fear says it would be sensible and more socially acceptable to just be quiet and let others speak. Fear often masquerades as sensibility, especially as we get older. Fear forgets what we have been given.

For you did not receive the spirit of slavery again to fall
back into fear, but you have received the spirit of adoption
as sons, by whom we cry, "Abba! Father!"
ROMANS 8:15

How often do we 'fall back' through fear? A 'fall back' is an easy place—a default. It's not a determined, indomitable action. The only way we can conquer fear is to decide to take God at His word; to decide that the outcome of our boldness is in God's hands (and not in the opinions of others).

Many of us are in that place today where we have been intimidated, bowed down to fear, and we wonder whether what we thought God had spoken over our lives was a figment of our imagination or actually real.

*The Lord is not slow in keeping His promises as
some understand slowness . . .*
2 PETER 3:9

Your future rests in a combination of heeding to the prophetic word over your life and believing what God has placed on your life will come to pass in His time.

*Father,
I choose to be defiant, to divide the lies from the truth, to stand my ground and to place and root my life in the will of God. I choose to live with uncompromised conviction and to speak the truth to powers and principalities. I choose to rest in the prophetic truth over my life. In Jesus' name, Amen.*

DECLARATION SIX

GOD INTERVENES ON MY BEHALF

*... It is because God has made me forget all my trouble
and all my father's household ... It is because God has
made me fruitful in the land of my suffering.*
GENESIS 41:51-52

Have you ever stood back and thought, 'I dodged a bullet there'? Have you ever looked at a situation that could have harmed you and realised that it ended up being fine—or better than fine?

This is the story and truth of our lives—what the enemy intended as a ploy, our God intended as a plan. What the enemy intended for evil, God works out as a master stroke of divine genius.

We have all dodged so many bullets.

In the passage of scripture, Joseph had gone through hell: abandonment and betrayal as well as injustice, yet God brought him out into a spacious place where he could declare the utter faithfulness of God.

Our past pain can contain us, unless we let God turn it around. God promises three things to help us in this today:

Firstly, divine forgetfulness. God promises us, as He did Joseph, that we would forget the trouble of our father's household; 'forget'—not in terms of a memory blackout but rather, the past not having any power over us. We can prophetically claim this forgetfulness today.

Secondly, God promises us divine fruitfulness. There is truly no experience, trauma or past reality that God can not use for His glory, if you let Him. God wants to bless your world however painful and restrictive it has been, and He wants to use it to create a testimony out of your tests and a message out of your mess.

And thirdly, God promises us divine authority. The amazing thing about the story of Joseph, is that after all that he had been through, he ended up second in charge over the whole land in which he suffered (Genesis 41:41-43). God promises us divine authority over that which we have experienced.

Joseph had seen so much pain, but God turned it all around. We have all had 'but God' moments in our past. And as prophetic beings, we need to stand on the promises of God to accelerate the journey of future 'but God' moments in our lives.

Father,
Help me to realise that when you are my Father, I do not have to remain at the mercy of my past but I am called to reign in life through Jesus Christ. Give me authority now over what has been my containment and confinement. Assure me again today of the plan you have for me. In Jesus' name, Amen.

DECLARATION SEVEN

THE TIME HAS COME!

This is the day the Lord has made; we will rejoice and be glad in it.
PSALM 118:24

There are some days when you just grasp hold of something: when an idea, a dream and a way forward finds itself in the palm of your hand. You're energised by God to grab a hold of that thing like you've not done in a long time, and run with it.

Today is that day. Prophesy it! Treat today as realignment—a reassignment—a new signpost to the dream and fresh attention on the miraculous potential that lies ahead.

A new boldness grips you to step out, to hold on and to run with what you have in your hand today.

You're back in the main game. Back on the agenda. You always knew you would be back, and today you are.

Time and time again, Joseph did this throughout his time in captivity—and the result was stunning!

Then Joseph said to his brothers, "Come close to me." When they had done so, he said, "I am your brother Joseph, the one you sold into Egypt! And now, do not be distressed and do not be angry with yourselves for selling me here, because it was to save lives that God sent me ahead of you. For two years now there has been famine in the land, and for the next five years there will be no ploughing and reaping. But God sent me

*ahead of you to preserve for you a remnant on earth and to
save your lives by a great deliverance. So then, it was not you
who sent me here, but God. He made me father to Pharaoh,
lord of his entire household and ruler of all Egypt."*

GENESIS 45:4-8

This is the moment when all of the hardship, all of the suffering and all of the loose ends were concluded by a master-stroke from Heaven—all because he took ahold of God from the very beginning.

Father,
Today I choose to let go of all excuses, all distractions and all fears. I choose to place my foot on the accelerator pedal and accelerate into all you've planned for my life. I accept my life, my future and my assignment and choose to celebrate it with all of my heart.
In Jesus' name, Amen.

DECLARATION EIGHT

GOD'S PLAN IS BIGGER!

Now the snake was more crafty than any of the wild animals the Lord God had made. He said to the woman, "Did God really say, 'you must not eat from any tree in the garden'?"

GENESIS 3:1

The enemy's job description is always to sow doubt over the plans of God, and he does it in your life; he will always try and downplay God's plan for your life. Our fight with the enemy is often exhausting and belittling.

You need to realise today that your fight is about something bigger than you. Your fight is for the future; the future of others as well as your legacy. It's about the Kingdom. It's about your children. It's about generations. It's so much bigger than you.

Sometimes we need to take a step back and realise the magnitude of what we are called to. We need a mindset in the midst of our everyday life that says these 'light and momentary troubles' we experience, hold within them 'a weight of glory that far outweighs them all.'

What happens to us when the enemy comes is that we compromise the plan of God for a moment of comfort and for a quiet life. Or we choose self-advancement over Kingdom-advancement, like Adam and Eve did in the garden.

When you are pregnant with a dream, when you can see the plan God has for you, a plan that is bigger than you and involves the deliverance of others, all hell can break out against you. At that point, we can often file that dream under 'this is too hard', and think to ourselves, 'it must not be the will of God any more'.

But the Bible tells us that God does not change His mind. It's time to stand up and fight—to fight for the plan of God for you and for those around you. It is so much bigger than us.

Father,
Thank you for the magnitude of the plan I am a part of. I refuse to believe the questions of the enemy any longer. I choose to stand and live by every word that proceeds out of the mouth of my God. I choose to rise up and move out in the power of the Spirit.
In Jesus' name, Amen.

DECLARATION NINE

I WALK IN MATURITY

They do not jostle each other; each marches straight ahead. They plunge through defences without breaking ranks.
JOEL 2:8

The day of jostling for position is over. It's time to deal a death blow to insecurities. It's time to take your place in an invincible, mature army where each person knows their place and their position. But that's not always easy. We need to move from a childish walk with God to an adult walk with God, from a slave of God mentality to an heir of God mentality.

What I am saying is that as long as an heir is under age, he is no different from a slave, although he owns the whole estate.
GALATIANS 4:1

The more 'adult' we become in our relationship with God, the more ownership of the ability to change a generation and ownership of the power of God Himself we have within our hands.

The Spirit you received does not make you slaves, so that you live in fear again; rather, the Spirit you received brought about your adoption to sonship.
ROMANS 8.15

Slaves approach their masters with fear. They're unsure of their future and have neither inheritance nor anything to pass on. Heirs inherit easily. Their legal standing makes it easy. Heirs have a secure relationship with the one from whom they will be receiving. They know that they have a special bond that no one else can emulate.

To boldly accept and take your inheritance is something children and slaves never do. It's time to grow up.

Father,
Today I take up my invitation to grow up and take my full rights and responsibilities as a citizen of Heaven. I choose to put on strength, fight my battles and receive by faith all I need to rise above what I face today. In Jesus' name, Amen.

DECLARATION TEN

WHAT I SEE, I SPEAK

*I pray that the eyes of your heart may be enlightened in order
that you may know the hope to which He has called you, the
riches of His glorious inheritance in His holy people, and His
incomparably great power for us who believe . . .*
EPHESIANS 1:18-19

The doorway to hope, the doorway to a love of His church and His
kingdom and the doorway to carrying great power all flow from the
eyes of our heart.

When the disciples saw Jesus walking on water, they looked at Him
through the eyes of their heads and not the eyes of their hearts, since
they didn't recognise Him. God is often at work in and around our lives
but we don't see Him; we are looking through the wrong set of eyes.

When the disciples recognised Jesus and invited Him into their boat,
they were immediately transported to their destination.

When Jacob was at Bethel, he humbly declared:

Surely the Lord is in this place and I was not aware of it.
GENESIS 28:16

God wants to open the eyes of our hearts to see His power, His
presence and His activity. He wants to give us prophetic, spiritual eyes
that deny the laws of the universe and see impossibility made possible
through the God of the universe.

When we see with the eyes of our heart, our spirit bypasses impossibility. We speak health over sickness. We speak provision over lack. We speak hope over disappointment.

We need to start choosing to see with our spiritual eyes, and ignore what we see with our natural eyes. We need to shut down our knee-jerk reactions to things that seem contrary to Jesus being in control. Today, in your hearts, choose to see that your God is 'working all things together for good'. (Romans 8:28)

Father,
Open the eyes of my heart that I might know you more dearly and clearly. Help me to realise the future hope to which I've been called and to really know the enormity of the power of God that's been made available to me through Christ's mighty resurrection.
In Jesus' name, Amen.

DECLARATION ELEVEN

I AM MORE THAN A CONQUEROR

What then shall we say in response to these things? If God is for us who can be against us? He who did not spare His own Son, but gave Him up for us all—how will He not also, along with Him, graciously give us all things? Who will bring any charge against those who God has chosen? It is God who justifies. Who then is the one who condemns? No one. Christ Jesus who died— more than that who was raised to life—is at the right hand of God and is also interceding for us. Who shall separate us from the love of Christ? Shall trouble or hardship or persecution or famine or nakedness or danger or sword?

ROMANS 8:31-35

So who is it that separates us from God? Who is it that interrupts our flow? Who is it that brings a charge? Who it is that allows the condemnation? No one but ourselves.

The scripture goes on to say, 'For I am convinced that neither death nor life, neither angels nor demons, neither the present or the future or any powers, neither height nor depth nor anything else in God's creation, will be able to separate us from the love of God that is in Christ Jesus our Lord.' (Romans 8:38)

We thought it was demons and we thought that maybe it was our own busyness making it impossible to touch God. But no. The whole time it was us: our posture, our attitude and our unbelief. We thought we had disappointed God, we thought we had failed, we thought we had not maintained momentum and we thought God didn't like us anymore. It was us all along!

The mistake we make is to think God's intrinsic closeness toward us changes because we are struggling.

God's word encompasses the whole gamut of life—'trouble, hardship, persecution, famine, nakedness, danger and sword'. He covers everything including a sense of famine in your soul and a sense of nakedness before God. The huge punch line from Heaven is found in the verse that follows -

No, in all these things we are more than
conquerors through Him who loved us.
ROMANS 8:37

The crucial point here is that God sees us as conquerors 'in the midst' of all our stuff, not after all of our stuff has subsided. He is not making the statement after the event, but right in the middle of our emotional state and our sense of exposure. He declares we are still seen as conquerors.

He sees you differently to how you see yourself; He sees your life through the lens of complete redemption and complete victory. He can do that because it is a victory He has already won for you.

Father,
Help me to see this. Help me to believe this and help me to act upon this. Help me to shrug off the lies of the enemy, to stop feeding the lies of rejection and abandonment, and start to see the power of my relationship with you. Thank you for your utter faithfulness towards me.
In Jesus' name, Amen.

DECLARATION TWELVE

I WEAR HIS SIGNET RING

*I will make you like a signet ring on my
finger, for I have chosen you.*
HAGGAI 2:23

Have you ever noticed that King Charles wears a signet ring on his little finger? It'd be tough to miss it. He fiddles endlessly with it when he is nervous. It's a seal signifying who he is and the office he holds. A signet ring is a personal seal and 'signature' of its owner.

This is a spectacular Bible verse that signifies our Father's ownership of us as His children. This promise of us as a signet ring on our Father's finger comes after an incredible call for the people of God to recommit to the magnificent obsession of serving humanity and the magnificent obsession of building the house of God.

It is a promise after a challenge. It is a call to once again attend to unfinished business—the unfinished business of awakening humanity to the love of God.

*'I am giving you a promise now while the seed is still in the barn.
You have not yet harvested your grain, and your grapevines, fig
trees, pomegranates, and olive trees have not yet produced their
crops. But from this day onward I will bless you.'*
HAGGAI 2:19

Today you stand on the brink of unfinished business and the Spirit of God is drawing you back to the place where you will dream again for the power of God to truly anoint your life and anoint all you do.

Our ability to do great things for God is not often hampered by our lack of desire for God, but more by our lack of confidence in His calling. Understanding your full potential in God is not always an easy thing to grasp. It's like a stream that is constantly being blocked up. Those beavers of life are constantly building dams in an attempt to stop you from realising this potential. There's the dam of insecurity, the dam of comparison, the dam of feeling overwhelmed as well as the dam of insignificance. It comes back to looking again at how God personally chose you from the very beginning.

> *Even before He made the world, God loved us and chose us in Christ to be holy and without fault in His eyes. God decided in advance to adopt us into His own family by bringing us to Himself by Christ Jesus. This is what He wanted to do and it gave Him great pleasure.*
> **EPHESIANS 1:4-5**

This is the time of our endorsement—our moment to understand the mandate upon us as His chosen ones. This is our time to take His ring, wear it with pride and rise into our call.

Father,
Thank you for choosing me and for appointing me for eternal purposes.
I accept my call and choose to rise up into it, no matter the cost. You are
magnificent, and I am humbled by your love and kindness.
In Jesus' name, Amen.

DECLARATION THIRTEEN

I AM STRONG IN SPIRIT

*And we know that in all things God works for the good of those
who love Him, who have been called according to His purpose.*
ROMANS 8:28

Life is a narrative, a journey, a story unfolding and an accumulation of feelings and chosen responses. And we are called to have a strong spirit throughout.

A strong spirit finds the 'all things working together for good' in the midst of life's twists and turns. A strong spirit finds the love of God when love has been taken away. It asks God to teach us, help us and uphold us. A strong spirit does not deny reality but applies faith and truth to the curve balls of life.

A strong spirit finds purpose when purpose has been taken away. It acknowledges the hand of God in the midst of trial and understands there is a purpose to everything. A strong spirit embraces with determination that 'all things work together for good', and refuses to be beaten.

Perseverance is often the vehicle to understanding the purposes of all you are going through. Trials make us broader people. Your trials are working for you a deeper and richer future, but you must mix into these both faith and patience.

*I consider that our present sufferings are not worth comparing
with the glory that will be revealed in us.*
ROMANS 8:18

A strong spirit embraces the fact that denial and hardship are creating a future glory that will soon be revealed.

It's our time to know the comfort of His presence and the magnificence of God's love. Today, take time to remember that He is always with you—every minute of every attitude, every mood swing and every action.

He will keep you strong to the end so that you will be free from all blame on the day when our Lord Jesus Christ returns. God will do this, for He is faithful to do what He says, and He has invited you into partnership with His Son, Jesus Christ our Lord.

1 CORINTHIANS 1:8-9

Father,
Open the eyes of my heart that I might believe deep down that everything will be more than OK. Give me a strong spirit and give me a confidence that you know what you're doing at all times in my life. I love you Lord and commit my life back into your hands. In Jesus' name, Amen.

DECLARATION FOURTEEN

I LIVE FOR A NOBLE CAUSE

But the noble make noble plans, and by noble deeds they stand.
ISAIAH 32:8

Today can be the resurrection of nobility—our opportunity to buy in again to a noble cause—a life lived bigger than our own wants and desires, nobility is not about how we look . . .

It's about kindness.

It's about integrity.

It's about justice, and it's about love.

It's about being an overcomer.

It's about being an optimist and it's about our glass always being half-full.

It's about a generous spirit and it's about a generous hand.

It's about living in the reality of the unseen.

It's about walking out the beauty of God's grace, and it's about walking in the light of eternity.

God's ability to look away and ignore offence has led you today into this noble cause in which you find yourself. You are also graced to be kind. Kindness is like the delicacy of a divine dessert; it leaves a beautiful taste in people's mouths. It is an olive branch that covers offence and a bridge that expands across the chasm between lives. Kindness continues to love when its efforts are not reciprocated. Today, may the power of Heaven ride on the back of your kind heart.

But the fruit of the spirit is love, joy, peace, patience, kindness, faithfulness, gentleness and self control . . .

GALATIANS 5:22-23

Our noble cause is to love people back to life, to exude kindness and optimism, to embrace the forgotten and to be an army of thoughtfulness for those who have been abandoned. Today, let us choose to live for a noble cause.

Father,
Help me to be a part of this revolution. Help me to trust that you hold my future in your hands and know that I am loved and prized by you. Energise me as I turn inside out and fill my life and the lives of others with beauty, kindness, grace and elegance. Help me live for the noble cause. In Jesus' name, Amen.

DECLARATION FIFTEEN

I CHOOSE VULNERABILITY

... to proclaim the year of The Lord's favour ...
ISAIAH 61:2

What a truth. We are favoured, and we proclaim it to those around us. Today is gear change time; it's transition time; it's time for the fulfilment of all those words previously spoken over you. In order to meet the full force of the favour of God though, we often have to go out on a limb of personal vulnerability.

That's what happened to Ruth. Ruth put herself in a place of great vulnerability to see the purposes of God unfold. Whether or not her advances to Boaz would attract rejection, abuse or humiliation, she lay herself at the feet of the purposes of God, trusting God to cover her vulnerability.

May you be richly rewarded by The Lord, the God of Israel, under whose wings you have come to take refuge.
RUTH 2:12

Vulnerability attracts God's favour because it's an act of giving away and giving up your own strength to God. It's time to be vulnerable about the real you, vulnerable to share your real opinions and vulnerable to do God's will when you feel ill equipped and poorly prepared—your God will reward your vulnerability richly!

The promises over you, the potential within you, the favour stored up for you, all rely on both your vulnerability and the boldness of your faith. If He says it, He will do it. End of story.

In the Psalms David often begins with his vulnerability and ends with God's covenant to cover him and protect him.

I am forgotten as though I were dead; I have become like broken pottery. For I hear many whispering, 'Terror on every side!' They conspire against me and plot to take my life. But I trust in you, Lord; I say, 'You are my God.' My times are in your hands; deliver me from the hands of my enemies, from those who pursue me. Let your face shine on your servant; save me in your unfailing love.

PSALM 31: 12-16

Your vulnerability is not your weakness, it's your invitation.

Father,
Even though it can feel uncomfortable stepping out and displaying my vulnerabilities to others around me, in dedication to your call, I choose to do just that and expect your strength and power to envelope me. Give me the spirit of power, love and a sound mind.
In Jesus' name, Amen.

DECLARATION SIXTEEN

WHAT GOD BEGINS, HE COMPLETES

I answered them by saying, "The God of Heaven will give us
success. We His servants will start rebuilding, but as for you, you
have no share in Jerusalem or any claim or historic right to it."
NEHEMIAH 2:20

When you start to build, your life will always attract opposition. This is a challenge not only of your resolve but of your security. It's the age old challenge of "did God say?". It's the jealousy of the non-builders wanting to deny the builders the right of building what they know to be right.

It's not time to argue or to be distracted by long discussions loaded in doubt and unbelief. It's time to affirm that this is not your battle, it's God's—and what God begins, He completes. God will give you success. Doubt has no place in faith, and 'doubters and mockers' have no place in sharing the exclusive preciousness of bringing Heaven to Earth.

The enemy always rides shotgun on the side of every dream. Be reminded of the greatness of all you're doing. Be reminded of the eternal consequences of the rebuilding work in your life and world.

Let us not become weary in doing good, for at the proper time we
will reap a harvest if we do not give up.
GALATIANS 6:9

Proper time' sounds boring but the 'proper time' is full of God. 'Proper time' unfolds the goodness, blessing and divine favour that the living God has for your life.

> *The Lord blessed the latter part of Job's life more than the*
> *former part. He had fourteen thousand sheep, six thousand*
> *camels, a thousand yoke of oxen and a thousand donkeys. And*
> *he also had seven sons and three daughters.*
> **JOB 42:12**

Let's never forget Job's 'proper time'—from nothing to everything, in God's timing.

Father,
I declare and proclaim that this is the season of the new build. This
is the season of being wide-eyed, alert and aware. This is the season
of new strategies. This is the season of placing the new wine into new
wineskins. Your word is true and all that You've begun in my life, You
will continue to the day of completion.
In Jesus' name, Amen.

DECLARATION SEVENTEEN

HE IS BUILDING A BEAUTIFUL HOUSE

"The glory of this present house will be greater than the glory of the former house," says The Lord Almighty ...
HAGGAI 2:9

God's Kingdom is not run by the solo performances of just a few individuals but every person—young and old, rich and poor, educated and uneducated, as well as people from every nation.

In the Book of Haggai, God called the Priest, the Governor and the people to all be involved: The Priest was to lead, the Governor was to govern, and the people were to contribute.

The enemy would tell you that you cannot contribute, and that others are doing more than you, and that what you can do is so small and insignificant. But that's not what the word of God says. God deals in the currency of breathing on small things and making them supernaturally significant.

When Jesus fed the five thousand, the little boy's parents who provided the loaves and fish didn't know when packing his lunch that day that it would be talked about thousands of years later. Their actions that day, and the way they had brought their son up in generosity, tapped into God's mighty power of multiplication.

God has the power to take one moment and make it history. God has the power to take our little and make it His best. Don't allow the enemy to disable you, devaluing your contribution by comparing it to the contribution of others. God's not looking for size, but excellence. Excellence is doing the best with what you have and with who you are.

It's through bite-size ministries that God will build His house. Our God has a beautiful habit of breathing on little offerings and supernaturally doing something amazing.

> *Father,*
> *You made water into wine by a little step of obedience and You parted the Red Sea by a small step of obedience. Help me to see what bite-size contribution I can give today and what step of obedience You'd like me to take to create both 'a beautiful house' and a miraculous future. In Jesus' name, Amen.*

DECLARATION EIGHTEEN

GOD REVEALS HIMSELF TO ME

... From now on I will tell you of new things, of hidden things unknown to you. They are created now, and not long ago. You have not heard of them before today. So you cannot say, yes I knew of them.

ISAIAH 48:6-7

This is the mystery of the new day, the next big thing and the expansive knowledge of God that He wants to draw us into.

We do not know what is out there, but our hearts hunger for that new thing, and God wants to take us there—the wonders of new experiences of God that are ours forever more.

The more you get to know God, the more you realise you never really knew Him before! It's the unfolding revelation of the nature, the power and the kindness of God, revealing something startling and new that takes our breath away.

Call to me and I will answer you, and tell you great and unsearchable things you do not know.

JEREMIAH 33:3

There is a new favour, influence, blessing and breakthrough that God wants to pour out upon you, yet the nature and form of it will be different to what you expect. The more we know God and His ways, the more we realise how they change from season to season and from event to event. Jesus only spat on a man's eyes once. He only turned water into wine once. The story's the same but His ways always change.

"For my thoughts are not your thoughts, neither are your ways my ways," declares the Lord. "As the Heavens are higher than the Earth, so are my ways higher than your ways and my thoughts than your thoughts. As the rain and the snow come down from Heaven, and do not return to it without watering the Earth and making it bud and flourish, so that it yields seed for the sower and bread for the eater, so is my word that goes out from my mouth: it will not return to me empty, but will accomplish what I desire and achieve the purpose for which I sent it. You will go out in joy and be led forth in peace; the mountains and hills will burst into song before you, and all the trees of the field will clap their hands."
ISAIAH 55:8-12

Expect the unexpected!

Father,
I am aware that for every emotion of frustration and impossibility in my life, there is a revealing of the nature of who You are. Show me something new today of Your ways, not just Your acts, so that I might know You more and live closer to Your heart.
In Jesus' name, Amen.

DECLARATION NINETEEN

I HAVE A NEW SOUND

*"'Watch me', he told them. "Follow my lead. When I get to the edge
of camp, do exactly as I do. When I and all who are with me blow
our trumpets, then from all around the camp blow yours, and
shout for the Lord and for Gideon.""*
JUDGES 7:17-18

Throughout the Bible, when a great change was about to come about there
was a new sound—a complete change of sound! In the New Testament,
just before the Holy Spirit was poured out there was a sound of a rushing
wind. In the first six days before the walls of Jericho came down there
was silence, yet on the seventh day they were instructed to raise a shout
and blow a trumpet. There was a change of sound. Gideon had been
on his way to fight the Midianites, then after a seeming narrowing of
his capability to win the battle, he raised a trumpet sound.

*'When the 300 trumpets sounded, the Lord caused the men
throughout the camp to turn on each other with their swords ...'*
JUDGES 7:22

There was an explosion of new sound, then an explosion of
breakthrough. There is always a new sound before a new move, whether
it's an unlocking of a dream, a new breakthrough or a new season.

For Gideon and his men, that sound was theirs to create. Let's follow their lead today and make a new sound. The sound of faith, of hope, of joy and of something new. Today marks the start of a radical change of sound in your life.

Paul and Silas changed the sound of their prison with the sound of praise. It proceeded the miraculous sound of God's power shaking the very foundations of where they stood. The same will happen to you as you change your sound.

'About midnight Paul and Silas were praying and singing hymns to God, and the other prisoners were listening to them. Suddenly there was such a violent earthquake that the foundations of the prison were shaken. At once all the prison doors flew open, and everyone's chains came loose.'

ACTS 16:25-26

Father,
Let my lifestyle, my habits, my dreams, my conversations and my prayer life begin to take on a new rhythm, a new melody and a new harmony with the things you've planned to come in to my life. Get me ready and make me a vital part of the change. Soften my heart and adapt my walk to come more in line with what you're about to do.
In Jesus' name, Amen.

DECLARATION TWENTY

MY WORDS ARE MY FUTURE

'From the fruit of their mouth a person's stomach is filled; with the harvest of their lips they are satisfied. The tongue has the power of life and death, and those who love it will eat its fruit.'
PROVERBS 18:20-21

One thing is for sure, the words of your mouth change when you encounter God! I have a friend in the UK whose nickname used to be 'Sarah Swearer'. She then had an encounter with God and her mouth cleaned up because of her new faith. After that, everything began to change, including her nickname.

Our future 'stepping into the new' requires that our mouths are cleaned up by the power of God. Not necessarily from actual swear words (though that may be helpful!) but from the words of doubt and smallness.

How often do we marginalise our future by the words of our mouth? Our future demands that our mouths are full of faith and declaration, not whining, whinging and fear.

My mum used to say, 'if you can't find anything nice to say, say nothing at all.'

If you can't find anything full of faith to say, say nothing at all. Shut up until you can discipline your mouth to only declare fresh downloads from Heaven. If our phones need to be updated regularly to get rid of the glitches in the previous operating systems, then it's even more true for ourselves.

It's time to spell out our future with a declaration of faith on our lips. Sometimes we just have to shut up, and then speak up once we have cleaned up our words and infused them with the Word of God.

'But the Lord said to me, "Do not say, 'I am too young.' You must go to everyone I send you to and say whatever I command you. Do not be afraid of them, for I am with you and will rescue you,' declares the Lord. Then the Lord reached out His hand and touched my mouth and said to me, "I have put my words in your mouth."'
JEREMIAH 1:7-9

Let the Word not just be in your heart, but let it be in your mouth.

Father,
Cause me to do just that. Let the Holy Spirit touch my lips and touch my tongue right now, purifying them of all their complaints and doubts. Help me to line up my heart with your Word and my thoughts with your thoughts.
In Jesus' name, Amen.

DECLARATION TWENTY-ONE

I LIVE IN A PLACE OF FAITH

'It was by faith that Abraham obeyed when God called him to leave home and go to another land that God would give him as an inheritance. He went without knowing where he was going. And even when he reached the land God promised him, he lived there by faith.'
HEBREWS 11:8-9

The Bible tells us that 'Abraham was like a foreigner living in tents'.

It's our calling to a life of faith that gives up sensibility and security to watch the invisible invade the visible. It's about being a people who know their residence is in Heaven and who know that this life is an opportunity to bring Heaven to Earth. It's about a people who long to do mighty exploits for God and don't settle for the 'normal'. God wants to take us somewhere and He needs to upset the apple cart to regain our attention.

'And so a whole nation came from this one man who was as good as dead—a nation with so many people that, like the stars in the sky and the sand on the seashore, there is no way to count them.'
HEBREWS 11:12

You were not designed to live in a place of permanence, but to live in a place of faith. God will move Heaven and Earth in your life to get you to a place of 'living in tents'. Tent dwellers are people who change quickly, move on seasonally and create mobility that sweeps Heaven to Earth.

Often, as soon as we try to build a house of permanence, the hurricane of circumstance seems to blow so strong that we're left with very little remaining.

God is trying to take us somewhere! God is trying to stop us being mesmerised by permanence and prevent us from being hypnotised by circumstance. He is calling us to the always-advancing, cutting edge of faith.

> *Father,*
> *I hear you. I am prepared for change. Today, I will stop looking for security in the things of this world; I am prepared to follow you. I choose to fix my eyes upon Jesus, the author and completer of my faith, and run the race that you've set before me. Please give me the strength. In Jesus' name, Amen.*

GOD IS DIVINE

'For to us a child is born, to us a Son is given, and the government will be on His shoulders. And He will be called Wonderful Counselor, Mighty God, Everlasting Father, Prince of Peace. Of the greatness of His government and peace there will be no end. He will reign on David's throne and over His Kingdom, establishing and upholding it with justice and righteousness from that time on and forever. The zeal of the Lord Almighty will accomplish this.'

ISAIAH 9:6-7

God starts above us—undaunted, incomparable and unbeatable. He is omnipresent, omnipotent and omniscient. He is everywhere, all-powerful and all-knowing. Yet He is not inactive in the affairs of either the entire world or the affairs of your own heart. He is currently making His enemies His footstool. He is currently causing mountains ahead of us to melt like wax before His presence. He is currently strengthening, moving, making progress, fighting, subduing and stretching out His arms to the humble.

He is divine. He reigns supreme.

DECLARATION TWENTY-TWO

STAND DOWN, DEVIL!

"'... Do not be afraid. Stand firm and you will see the deliverance the Lord will bring you today. The Egyptians you see today you will never see again. The Lord will fight for you, you need only to be still." Then the Lord said to Moses, "Why are you crying out to me? Tell the Israelites to move on. Raise your staff and stretch out your hand over the sea to divide the water so that the Israelites can go through the sea on dry ground."'

EXODUS 14:13-16

Sometimes we think that crying out to God is all that we can do in a situation. And sometimes it is. But sometimes, it's not. Sometimes we need to speak the Word of God over our bondage and tell it to shift in Jesus' name!

Moses had to speak out, raise his staff and stretch out his hand. He had to raise his voice as well as raise his staff, which represented the power of God, and stretch it out in faith over the unknown and the impossible.

Today, you need to raise your voice and tell the voices of despair, discouragement and pessimism to stand down in Jesus' name. Place the power of the Word of God on your lips and declare His great deliverance over the cruel bondage you might find yourself in.

Then walk out of where you are and stretch out in faith to pursue God's purpose like you've never pursued it in all of the history of your life.

Today, God is going to lift the bondage over your mind, over your family and over your world, in Jesus' name!

'I will say of the Lord, "He is my refuge and my fortress, my God, in whom I trust." Surely He will save you from the fowler's snare and from the deadly pestilence. He will cover you with His feathers, and under His wings you will find refuge; His faithfulness will be your shield and rampart. You will not fear the terror of night, nor the arrow that flies by day, nor the pestilence that stalks in the darkness, nor the plague that destroys at midday. A thousand may fall at your side, ten thousand at your right hand, but it will not come near you.'
PSALM 91:2-7

Every breakthrough begins with, 'I will say of the Lord'. It's time to receive boldness from God and take a stand upon His Word today.

Father,
Let the Spirit be mine. Baptise me in boldness and courage and enable me to stop nursing my inferiorities and disappointments, and to rise above it in expectation of the works of God in my life. I choose to be like Moses and speak up and stretch out into the possibilities of Heaven. In Jesus' name, Amen.

DECLARATION TWENTY-THREE

I'M TAKING MY TERRITORY!

'Then the Lord will drive out all these nations before you, and you will dispossess nations larger and stronger than you. Every place where you set your foot will be yours: your territory will extend from the desert to Lebanon, and from the Euphrates River to the Mediterranean Sea. No one will be able to stand against you. The Lord your God, as He promised you, will put the terror and fear of you on the whole land wherever you go.'

DEUTERONOMY 11:23-25

Not understanding the permission Heaven has granted to us is one of the greatest barriers to setting our feet upon that which God wants to give us. You actually have the permission of Heaven to advance. It's yours for the taking. It is the ploy of the enemy to prevent you from understanding the authority you actually have for the land you're called to inhabit.

The issue is not a lack of territory—the issue is not seeing it as yours! Sometimes our past can make us blind to seeing what future territory lies ahead of us.

The Book of Joshua starts with the stark statement, 'Moses is dead.' In other words, the successes and failures of the past were over. And it's the same for you—it's time for you to pave a way into your allotted territory by moving on from where you were in the past.

The relationship that got you through your previous season—consider it dead. The connection that got you from A to B, consider that dead.

The friendship that supported you in your winter time—consider it dead. The way you did life while you were just holding on—consider that dead too. And the victories you've won and medals you've received are both so yesterday! Consider them all dead and gone.

Sometimes dead is good.

'... *unless a kernel of wheat falls to the ground and dies it remains only a single seed. But if it dies it produces many seeds.*'
JOHN 12:24

It's time to let go of the former things and claim the specific territory that God has marked out for you.

Father,
I declare that today is my day for occupation. It's the day to bury my Moses and move on into my inheritance. It is my day to see the full extent of my allotted territory that was won for me upon your cross. Give me faith to reach out, move on forward, and take my place in history. I know that a generation waits for it.
In Jesus' name, Amen.

DECLARATION TWENTY-FOUR

THERE IS MERCY IN THE MIDDLE

'... So that by His death He might destroy him who holds the power of death—that is the devil—and free those who all their lives were held in slavery by their fear of death.'
HEBREWS 2:14-15

When reading again the story of the death of Jesus and His amazing resurrection, I had forgotten that there were three days in the middle when there was an apparent silence. It was a block of time when Heaven went silent and when it seemed like the victory had not been won.

When Jesus died, however, the resurrection was already in His mind. The outcome was certain, yet for three days it appeared that all was lost. Jesus was busy at this juncture in time, at this middle-point, but to all intent and purposes it looked like the game was over.

Right in the silence of the grave, however, was the purchase of a redemption so powerful that it would turn the course of mankind forever.

There is freedom being purchased for you today in the silence of your current moment.

God hears your cry today and even though you may not see the outcome in the current silence, He sees it and is working non-stop to see it come to pass. There is mercy in the middle of our journey, even when we rant and rave and stand on our heads to try to force the hand of God to move! He understands our humanity. He understands that the middle is a difficult place to be.

'For we do not have a high priest who is unable to empathise with our weaknesses, but we have one who has been tempted in every way, just as we are—yet He did not sin. Let us then approach the throne of grace with confidence, so that we may receive mercy and find grace to help us in our time of need.'

HEBREWS 4:15-16

He covers our fears, our lack of trust and our propensity to develop a plan B. He gives us mercy in the middle. Today, if you feel like you are in the middle of something, know that there is mercy for you from Heaven. But more than that, know that God is busy working a miracle on your behalf.

Father,
I realise today that you are always present, always at work, always looking, always leading and always on my side. Help me to love your heart before your hand, and help me to trust that you know what you're doing. I decide to trust in you and believe that I'm the right person in the right place at the right time and that, even though I sometimes live in silence, you are working for me right now to see my deliverance and my victory.
In Jesus' name, Amen.

DECLARATION TWENTY-FIVE

HE'S THE GOD OF TRANSFORMATION

*'Restore our fortunes, Lord, as streams renew the desert. Those
who plant in tears will harvest with shouts of joy.'*
PSALM 126:4-5

Streams in the Negev are streams in the desert that come after torrential
rain. They literally transform a barren place into a place with beautiful
flowers and wildlife. This is not just about joy, this is about harvest.

Your God is a specialist in breathing over nothing and creating
everything. Nothing does not mean defeat. It actually means the creation
of space for God to breathe. We sometimes feel like there's an organised
onslaught on our lives with the powers of the enemy trying to dismantle
us and break us down on every side. What's really going on is that God
is using this to break us and to remould us into even more powerful
vessels. He is rearranging the furniture.

Brokenness before God is not a turn off. Our hearts at times think
that God is only attracted to the perfect and the fully formed. God the
Holy Spirit is magnetically attracted to both brokenness and despair.
God is not a God who only provides for the capable. God is a God
who provides oil for the incapable and, through His anointing, makes
them capable.

Isaiah 61 is a passage that Jesus quoted when outlining the kind of
ministry that God specialises in. And it's all about transformation. Selah.

'The Spirit of the Sovereign Lord is on me, because the Lord has anointed me to proclaim good news to the poor.
He has sent me to bind up the broken-hearted, to proclaim freedom for the captives and release from darkness for the prisoners, to proclaim the year of the Lord's favour and the day of vengeance of our God, to comfort all who mourn, and provide for those who grieve in Zion—to bestow on them a crown of beauty instead of ashes, the oil of joy instead of mourning, and a garment of praise instead of a spirit of despair. They will be called oaks of righteousness, a planting of the Lord for the display of His splendour. They will rebuild the ancient ruins and restore the places long devastated; they will renew the ruined cities that have been devastated for generations. Strangers will shepherd your flocks; foreigners will work your fields and vineyards. And you will be called priests of the Lord, you will be named ministers of our God. You will feed on the wealth of nations, and in their riches you will boast.'

ISAIAH 61:1-6

It's time for your restoration, your rebuilding, your re-invention and re-alignment according to God's amazing plans and purposes for your life.

Father,
After all these years of running on empty and having very little powder left in the cannon, I now turn to the God of my transformation. Give me the spirit of wisdom and understanding to know your ways and to see that deep within me, you weren't trying to destroy me but create me—the next me—the me that's ready to meet with the blessings and victories as well as the position of responsibility you have planned for my life. In Jesus' name, Amen.

DECLARATION TWENTY-SIX

HE WILL RESTORE WHAT WAS LOST

*'The Lord says, "I will give you back what you lost to the swarming
locusts, the hopping locusts, the stripping locusts, and the cutting
locusts. It was I that sent this great destroying army against you.
Once again you will have all the food you want, and you will
praise The Lord your God, who does these miracles for you ... "'*

JOEL 2:25-26

God is a God of restoration. He finds things that are lost, and fixes
things that are broken. Today God promises that He will restore to
you what you had.

What did you once have that you lost or mislaid in the sheer pace
of life? What have you put down but can't find again to pick back up?

The trouble with losing something is that you never know where
you lost it—if you did it wouldn't be lost! The Word of God clearly
states, 'I will give you back what you lost'. He knows where you lost it.

God will restore to you the years the locust have eaten. He will
restore to you your youth and give you back the skip in your step. He
will restore that place, that level, that security, that position and that
promise that He had already given to you.

The joy and the wonder of your yesterday is the first promise of your
today. Don't let anybody tell you your yesterdays are of no importance
to God. He values every memory and every moment of beauty. He sees
every moment of sheer joy and every place where these things were

lost into the sea of grief and pain. Your tears are remembered and your restoration is guaranteed.

This is what happened to Job.

'*The Lord blessed the latter part of Job's life more than the former part. He had fourteen thousand sheep, six thousand camels, a thousand yoke of oxen and a thousand donkeys. And he also had seven sons and three daughters. The first daughter he named Jemimah, the second Keziah and the third Keren-Happuch. Nowhere in all the land were there found women as beautiful as Job's daughters, and their father granted them an inheritance along with their brothers. After this, Job lived a hundred and forty years; he saw his children and their children to the fourth generation. And so Job died, an old man and full of years.*'

JOB 42:12-16

He's about to restore to you the stolen years.

Father,
Cause me to take hold of this truth. Cause me to change my feelings of regret and exchange them for feelings of joy. I believe your Word and, like Job, I believe that my God has the power to restore all that has been lost. Allow me the faith to dream again.
In Jesus' name, Amen.

DECLARATION TWENTY-SEVEN

THERE IS MORE BESIDES!

'Return to the stronghold, O prisoners who have the hope; this
very day I am declaring that I will restore double to you.'
ZECHARIAH 9:12

'... The Lord restored his fortunes. In fact the
Lord gave him twice as much as before!'
JOB 42:10

The wonderful beauty about our God is that He is the God of the increase.
His restoration involves not just the giving back of that which was stolen,
lost or thrown away, but the doubling of it. God is the God of the very
much more. Personally, in your life, He promises ever increasing joy
and ever increasing glory.

'On that day I will gather you together and bring you home
again. I will give you a good name, a name of distinction
among the nations of the Earth, as I restore your fortunes
before their very eyes. I, the Lord, have spoken!'
ZEPHANIAH 3:20

Along with restoration, God also promises a name of distinction—a
turn around of your reputation for all whose name has been dragged
through the mud—when you have been totally misunderstood and
misjudged.

The wonderful thing with all this restoration is that all of it is completely and exclusively the hand of God. It is not something that you can strive for. He prophetically speaks over your life today.

For those who have stood their ground—this is the promise of God. This 'good name' is a name God will give you. It's got nothing to do with your effort. This distinction is God-given not publicity manufactured. Today, you can leave it all to the Spirit of the living God.

> *Father,*
> *I have been so aware of what others have or might be saying about me and the reputation I've picked up. I am amazed by your ability to restore and give back more than was even taken away, including my good name.*
> *In Jesus' name, Amen.*

DECLARATION TWENTY-EIGHT

I HAVE A HOLY CALLING

'The one who calls you is faithful, and He will do it.'
1 THESSALONIANS 5:24

You have been called by God Himself—not by a queen nor a king, but by the Creator of the Universe and the 'Author and Perfector of your faith'. This means so much.

Firstly, it means that you cannot fail—you didn't choose God, He chose you. Your life isn't primarily built on your faithfulness nor your ability to lay ahold of your future, it's built on His faithfulness and His ability to lay hold of both you and your future.

Secondly, it means that you won't be left stranded halfway through your journey. He provides for those He calls—where there is a vision, there is also provision.

And thirdly, it means that it's not off-the-shelf—it's tailor made by the King of Heaven, just for you.

Not long ago, the Holy Spirit said to me, 'you underestimate the uniqueness of your calling. You need to value your distinctiveness.'

For everyone:

Our calling is to be a part of the great rescue.

Our calling is to defy the boundaries of the impossible. Our calling is to bring freedom to those who are oppressed.

Our calling is to speak on behalf of those who have no voice. Our calling is to touch humanity with the love of God.

Our calling is to silence the limitations of our yesterday. Our calling is to prophesy a new word over our tomorrow.

Yet within all of this lies a specific calling for which God has graced us for. The sky is not the limit. Our beautiful, bountiful calling is. Let's walk the length and breadth of it today.

Father,
Let me have the revelation that I have been called not by a queen or king, and not by a president or prime minister, but by the King of Kings. Help me to see the incredible honour involved and help me to treat it with all of the honour that's due.
In Jesus' name, Amen.

DECLARATION TWENTY-NINE

YOU HAVE SAVED THE BEST FOR NOW

> *'Everyone brings out the choice wine first and then the*
> *cheaper wine after the guests have had too much to*
> *drink; but you have saved the best till now.'*
>
> **JOHN 2:10**

Our God is a God who operates in 'ever-increasing glory.'

So often the reason we personally see less and less in our lives and world, is that we settle for yesterday's moves of God and don't believe that God has the better wine and better moves to come.

We end up spending all of our time trying to look respectable to cover up the increasing lack within. There wasn't one moment when Jesus' mission was to look respectable to anybody; His life was about advancement and nothing else.

> *'Nearby stood six stone water jars, the kind you find used*
> *by the Jews for ceremonial washing, each holding from*
> *twenty to thirty gallons. Jesus said to the servants, "Fill*
> *the jars with water", so they filled them to the brim.'*
>
> **JOHN 2:6-7**

Jesus could have created wine from nothing. But He didn't because He wanted to involve the servants in the miracle. The way to do that was through the strange faith action of filling ordinary stone jars with water.

Lack demanded faith and action.

The stone jars in front of you right now are the keys to your 'ever-increasing' from God.

It's truly amazing that Jesus created the choicest wine out of something so plain.

Our God wants to pour out the new, the miraculous and the much more in your coming season. There is a whole new season and ministry for your life unlike that which you have lived. Allow today to be the day where you choose to fill your ordinary-looking stone jars with faith and prophesy your miracle.

Father,
I choose today to take a hold of the faith life and get involved in creating
the new season that you have for me. Help me not to lament over the
running out of 'wine' in my life, but help me to see it as a stitch up for
the next big thing. I thank you that out of 'your glorious riches' you will
take me into my next stage of fruition and blessing.
In Jesus' name, Amen.

DECLARATION THIRTY

I'M EXTENDING MY BORDERS

*'He brought me out into a spacious place; He
rescued me because He delighted in me.'*
PSALM 18:19

TV programmes about people buying new homes are driven by a quest for more space; people always want something bigger than what they currently have. It's a cry within our spirits that goes way beyond just a bigger house. Our inner self longs for a bigger world with room to expand, extend and grown into. We're born to grow.

We want God to breathe over our little and create something spacious and breath-taking.

That is exactly what your God wants to do in you today. He is hovering over your waters of smallness right now and is poised to act on your behalf.

It's time not just to focus on the fact that He rescues you and He loves you—sometimes smallness of thinking keeps us in that second part of the scripture. It's time to really lay claim to the first part of the verse—'He brought me out into a spacious place'.

God's intention for you has always been a spacious place.

It's time to expand into it.

Isaiah 54 speaks about a woman who was unable to have children, but was able to create a spacious place in anticipation for what God was about to do. This needs to be a foundational passage for your life as well.

*"'Sing, barren woman, you who never bore a child; burst
into song, shout for joy, you who were never in labour;
because more are the children of the desolate woman than
of her who has a husband," says the Lord. "Enlarge the
place of your tent, stretch your tent curtains wide, do not
hold back; lengthen your cords, strengthen your stakes.
For you will spread out to the right and to the left; your
descendants will dispossess nations and settle in their desolate
cities. Do not be afraid; you will not be put to shame. Do not
fear disgrace; you will not be humiliated. You will forget the
shame of your youth and remember no more the reproach of
your widowhood. For your Maker is your husband—the Lord
Almighty is His name—the Holy One of Israel is your Redeemer;
He is called the God of all the earth. The Lord will call you back
as if you were a wife deserted and distressed in spirit—a wife who
married young, only to be rejected," says your God.'*

ISAIAH 54:1-6

It's time to stretch out and prepare for what's to come.

*Father,
I accept your invitation to extend the borders of my spirit and confront
the borders of fear, intimidation and religion in my life. Give me the
power to have my Isaiah 54 season of extending my 'tent' so wide that
I prepare the way for the fruitfulness that's coming my way. Thank you
for delighting in me always.
In Jesus' name, Amen.*

DECLARATION THIRTY-ONE

IT'S MOVING DAY!

'Crowds of sick people—blind, lame, or paralyzed—lay on the porches. One of the men lying there had been sick for thirty-eight years. When Jesus saw him and knew he had been ill for a long time, He asked him, "Would you like to get well?". "I can't, sir," the sick man said, "for I have no one to put me into the pool when the water bubbles up. Someone else always gets there ahead of me." Jesus told him, "Stand up, pick up your mat, and walk!" Instantly, the man was healed! He rolled up his sleeping mat and began walking.'

JOHN 5:3-9

We read about a man who had been paralysed and put in a place filled with sickness, smallness and tightness of space for up to 38 years. He had spent a lifetime of watching disputes and hostility, as well as watching others steal away his desire. Then, out of the blue, Jesus came along and said this is moving day. It was time to move.

It's the same thing with you. It's time to walk out of where you've been surviving and into your prophesied future—your spacious place.

It's easy to sit around a pool that represents the security of just getting by. This man had spent up to 38 years watching a pool that literally reflected his brokenness. It was only when he looked up at Jesus and took hold of his miracle that everything changed.

God wants to take you and your life into much broader horizons. He wants to take you along a path you have never been before. The pool may feel secure, but it's not where God wants you to stay. As we have already declared -

> *'Enlarge your house, build an addition. Spread out your home, and spare no expense! For you will soon be bursting at the seams. Your descendants will occupy other nations and resettle ruined cities.'*
> ### ISAIAH 54:2-3

The old season is constantly calling you back but the new season is redesigning you for a bigger faith.

We need to align ourselves with the programme: fearless, spacious and large with no restriction! Let's begin with us and then take it to the world.

> *Father,*
> *I am choosing to move today to a place where my cautious becomes deliciously reckless—place where my weakness becomes undeniably strong and where my doubt is replaced by undaunting faith. This is my moving day from sin to forgiveness, from sickness to health and from restriction to space. This is my inheritance and this is my future. In Jesus' name, Amen.*

DECLARATION THIRTY-TWO

DON'T MESS WITH THE MUSTARD!

'Truly I tell you, if you have faith as small as a mustard seed,
you can say to this mountain, "Move from here to there," and
it will move. Nothing will be impossible for you.'
MATTHEW 17:20

Mustard seeds are the small round seeds of various mustard plants. They are usually around 1 to 2 millimetres in diameter and are coloured from yellowish white to black. These seeds all produce mustard; there's Yellow Mustard, Honey Mustard, Spicy Brown Mustard, Dijon Mustard, Whole Grain Mustard, Hot Mustard, English Mustard, German Mustard as well as French Mustard. They're all different kinds of mustard yet they are all mustard.

Your faith is just like someone else's faith, yet it's different to other people's faith—it has a different purpose, a different outcome and a different way of doing things. It's unique; it's yours. And it will be used by God in all sorts of different ways. God is quite capable of using the seemingly small deposit inside of you and making dishes of power that move mountains and part the seas.

Your journey of faith will appear different to anyone else's experience. Do not dismiss it. Don't put on anyone else's armour—operate out of your own special brand of faith that God has given you.

Many of us have been pushed into a faithless corner because the enormity of someone else's expression of faith has stopped our own transaction of faith.

Don't let anyone mock your mustard and don't let anyone mess with your mustard. God knows that sometimes you feel like you have little faith, but that is all you need. The Holy Spirit works with mustard seeds. He does miracles with mustard seeds, and He only needs the little faith you dismiss as nothing, to create everything.

Father,
I thank you for my mustard seed of faith. Thank you for all of the dishes that you have chosen to make out of the mustard I possess. I will no longer compare my seed with anyone else's seed, or my future dishes with theirs. I possess a seed of power and I'm confident in the ability of the Masterchef who's at work in both the kitchen of my heart and the kitchen of Heaven.
In Jesus' name, Amen.

DECLARATION THIRTY-THREE

HIS WAYS ARE HIGHER

*'Then The Lord said to Moses, "Tell the Israelites to turn back
and camp near Pi Hahiroth, between Migdol and the sea. They
are to encamp by the sea, directly opposite **Baal Zephon.**"'*
EXODUS 14:1-2

Sometimes, the right thing to do is not to press on forward, but it's to actually turn back and trust!

This is so hard to swallow. We are used to advancement and we disdain any act of retreat. We think we know how to do this victory thing, even though things are much more difficult than they ought to be.

God's ways are higher than our ways. Look at the next couple of verses:

*'Pharaoh will think, "The Israelites are wandering around
the land in confusion, hemmed in by the desert." And I will
harden Pharaoh's heart, and he will pursue them.
But I will gain glory for myself through Pharaoh and all his
army, and the Egyptians will know that I am the Lord . . . '*
EXODUS 14:3-4

God had devised a plan whereby the enemy that was chasing them down was to be confused by the inexplicable retreat of the Israelites.

The truth is that God has devised a victory for your life that defies the natural order of things.

We need, however, to wise up!

We need to never embrace Pharaoh's thinking. Pharaoh was meant to think the Israelites were wandering around in confusion. The goal was for Pharaoh to think they were lost and vulnerable. It was not, however, for the Israelites to think like Pharaoh. It was not for them to think they were lost and vulnerable. It was a trick—a strategic attack against Pharaoh.

These thoughts were meant for Pharaoh, not for you. Confusion is not your inheritance. It's time to trust that God knows best through all of the unexpected change.

Father,
I can see that things are changing and I know that my ways are not
your ways. I choose to trust that you know best! Help me not to take on
the thinking of Pharaoh. Help me to know that your role is to outsmart
my enemies and to make a footstool out of them. I choose to move out
in faith and not be shaken by the change around me. I choose to rise
up in faith and get ready to cross my Red Sea and enter into my future.
In Jesus' name, Amen.

DECLARATION THIRTY-FOUR

THIS IS MY MOMENT

'Then Peter stood up with the Eleven, raised
his voice and addressed the crowd...'
ACTS 2:14

Here we see the moment of destiny that redefined Peter from restored coward to reformed apostle, ready to change the world. This moment was purposed and planned by the Creator of Heaven and Earth, and He has the same in store for you.

You are not here at this moment in this pocket of history because of a random God thought. It is your moment of destiny. You could have been born at any time in history yet, God has placed you at this juncture. God has worked hard to get you here. It's not by chance; it's by the hand of Heaven.

Even Jesus had to negotiate a journey that threatened His existence to get to His moment in time. Some of us have been through huge trauma and suffered things that no one should ever have to and yet, you are still here.

God has ordained your life to count at this moment in time. It is the ploy of the enemy to undermine and belittle your importance to God's unfolding of history. Esther almost missed her place in history until she was reminded:

'For if you remain silent at this time, relief and deliverance
for the Jews will arise from another place, but you and your
father's family will perish. And who knows but that you
have come to your royal position for such a time as this?'

ESTHER 4:14

It was this proclamation that saved a generation. Esther rose into her destiny.

Your placement at this moment, in the life you are living, is crucial. You've been brought to the Kingdom for such a time as this. Don't hide away. Rise up and be all you were called to be.

Father,
Thank you. I choose to never undermine my calling and significance again. I may never be famous but I am called to be significant to my generation. Cause me to maximise my call and rise into all you have set aside for my life.
In Jesus' name, Amen.

DECLARATION THIRTY-FIVE

IT'S MY BIRTHRIGHT

'Therefore, say to the Israelites: "I am the Lord, and I will
bring you out from under the yoke of the Egyptians. I will
free you from being slaves to them, and I will redeem you
with an outstretched arm and with mighty acts of judgment.
I will take you as my own people, and I will be your God.
Then you will know that I am the Lord your God, who
brought you out from under the yoke of the Egyptians."'

EXODUS 6:6-7

When God promised deliverance through Moses to save the people of God out of bondage, the people measured their response through filters that they had consciously or unconsciously embraced over a long period of time. They responded to God through a blanket of discouragement and the pain of their bondage.

We too can succumb to our oppression and accept the status quo of our experience rather than keep reaching for the possibilities of our future.

The Israelites were God's own people—freedom was their birthright, but they struggled to take God at His word because of where they found themselves. They were deeply settled in their bondage.

We need to learn to stand out as people who actually believe what God has promised—that He is a God of miracles, that He is alive and well, and that He will reward those who diligently seek Him.

We need to reinstate the strong minded optimism that is the currency of faith. We can be sure that no matter what people tell us, or what games the world plays, our God is seated on the throne.

Cut faith with a knife and it bleeds an expectation that something good is about to happen in your world. It bleeds hope. In the book of Hebrews, it says that 'faith is the foundation of everything hoped for.'

'... how much more will those who receive God's abundant
provision of grace and of the gift of righteousness reign in
life through the one man, Jesus Christ!'
ROMANS 5:17

Today, it's time for you to let go of all that's held you back, take God at His word, and reign. It's your birthright.

Father,
Help me to shrug off all of my disappointment and fear and grasp with both hands the deliverance you have for me. Help me to look up, see my salvation and declare your promises from this time forward.
In Jesus' name, Amen.

DECLARATION THIRTY-SIX

THERES'S A SOUND OF GENEROSITY

*'A generous person will prosper; whoever refreshes
others will himself be refreshed.'*
PROVERBS 11:25

The prosperity of your future and the ability of God to pour out the abundance of Heaven upon you directly relates to your decision to create a the sound of generosity.

I'll never forget, as a child, the open wooden offering plates that went round church at a particular time in the service, where the sound of coins clinking onto the wood would echo around the stone walls.

Numerous times through the years, when our church was in lack, a decision was made to give away the whole of a Sunday's offering to either the local community or to projects that helped the poor and the broken, believing in faith that God would provide. And He always did.

The commitment of a generous life is seen in the constant search for ways to be generous. It's a search to go the extra mile with people; to lay down your personal desires and wants for others; to be the first to pay when you're out for a meal, and to be mindful of those who have both succeeded or failed so that your words can encourage and lift.

And when it's not reciprocated, it's immediately time to move into double generosity—proving to all that you did it all with no strings attached and no small print added.

Generosity speaks volumes. Today, let's be purposeful in turning up the sound of our generosity.

'Remember this: whoever sows sparingly will also reap sparingly, and whoever sows generously will also reap generously. Each of you should give what you have decided in your heart to give, not reluctantly or under compulsion, for God loves a cheerful giver. And God is able to bless you abundantly, so that in all things at all times, having all that you need, you will abound in every good work. As it is written: "They have freely scattered their gifts to the poor; their righteousness endures for ever." Now He who supplies seed to the sower and bread for food will also supply and increase your store of seed and will enlarge the harvest of your righteousness. You will be enriched in every way so that you can be generous on every occasion, and through us your generosity will result in thanksgiving to God.'

2 CORINTHIANS 9:6-11

How many promises are wrapped around the noise that the generous make!

Father,
Give to me a generous spirit. Help me to trust you over my own resources, as I now look to resource others. Help me to be strategic in generosity, thoughtful, and mindful of everyone around me. Continue to give me a heart for both the poor and needy, and those forgotten in the hustle and bustle of life.
In Jesus' name, Amen.

DECLARATION THIRTY-SEVEN

I EMBRACE THE STRETCH

*'Then the angel of God, who had been traveling in front of
Israel's army, withdrew and went behind them. The pillar
of cloud also moved from in front and stood behind them,
coming between the armies of Egypt and Israel.
Throughout the night the cloud brought darkness to the one
side and light to the other side; so neither went near the other
all night long. Then Moses stretched out his hand over the
sea, and all that night the Lord drove the sea back with a
strong east wind and turned it into dry land. The waters were
divided, and the Israelites went through the sea on dry ground,
with a wall of water on their right and on their left.'*
EXODUS 14:19-22

Things change when you begin to speak out, raise your staff and stretch out your hand like Moses did when he found himself in the midst of impossibility.

In this story we see the position of God actually changes. The angel of God moved from in front of Moses and the children of God, and went behind them. Even the tangible pillar of cloud to which the people had become accustomed to seeing up ahead of them had moved behind them.

When God moves like this He is distancing you from your past, your history and your failures as well as your successes. He then waits for the stretch when you lean over your future and move into your deliverance.

At this point, Moses stretched out his hand over the sea and over the impossible. The waters divided and a smooth path of deliverance miraculously appeared before him.

There is a change in the spiritual climate when we straighten our back, speak up, raise our staff and stretch out our hand. God changes His stance and His position. It's then that we see the miraculous deliverance from bondage to freedom.

Paul knew all about the power of the stretch. This is his declaration:

'Not that I have already obtained all this, or have already arrived at my goal, but I press on to take hold of that for which Christ Jesus took hold of me. Brothers and sisters, I do not consider myself yet to have taken hold of it. But one thing I do: forgetting what is behind and straining towards what is ahead, I press on towards the goal to win the prize for which God has called me heavenwards in Christ Jesus.'

PHILIPPIANS 3:12-14

Let God give you a forward memory that is filled with what He's about to do in your life as you stretch out.

Father,
I'm getting it. I can't stay in the grip of fear and resentment. I believe that this is my time to speak out my future, raise up the staff of my authority and stretch it out in prayer and declaration towards my future. I thank you for this new spirit of prophecy that's falling upon me.
In Jesus' name, Amen.

DECLARATION THIRTY-EIGHT

THERE'S POWER IN MY VISION

'"... What shall we do?" the servant asked. "Don't be afraid," the prophet answered. "Those who are with us are more than those who are with them." And Elisha prayed, "Open his eyes, Lord, so that he may see." Then The Lord opened the servant's eyes, and he looked and saw the hills full of horses and chariots of fire all around Elisha.'

2 KINGS 6:15-17

In 2 Kings 6 we read the story of Elisha up against the King of Aram. The king was angry as Elisha always seemed to be one step ahead of him.

There is a lot to be said to understanding what is real and what is not, but in this passage we see that there are two realities in play—and these two realities play out in our lives all of the time.

Firstly, it was very clear that Elisha saw the physical reality of where he found himself—he saw that he was surrounded by an army of impossibility. It is silly not to recognise what can be clearly seen around about our lives.

But then, to make a way for God to move, Elisha called for the servant to see what was actually going on, and to see with his spiritual eyes the actual truth of the situation—the spiritual reality.

Elisha knew that he was going to be OK because he saw the spiritual reality in the midst of this physical reality. He saw the hills full of the horses and the chariots symbolising God's divine power over the enemy.

To look at a situation purely through natural vision is to deny God's supernatural involvement with our lives. Even in the darkest moments of our lives, God is working all things together for our good.

'... *He who began a good work in you*
will carry it on to completion ...'
PHILIPPIANS 1:6

God completes what He starts, and He continues today by opening your eyes to see His total involvement and commitment to your victorious future.

Father,
Help us to see today that 'greater is He who is in me than he who is in the world'. Help us to not escape from our obvious troubles and trials but to live above them through our faith that our God is able and our God is greater.
In Jesus' name, Amen.

DECLARATION THIRTY-NINE

I'M ON A ROAD LESS TRAVELLED

*'I will lead the blind by ways they have not known, along
unfamiliar paths I will guide them; I will turn the darkness
into light before them and make the rough places smooth . . . '*
ISAIAH 42:16

Sometimes we confuse unfamiliarity with being off course. Just because you don't recognise the road you are currently on does not mean you are lost. We need to learn to see with eyes of the Spirit, before we see the outcome of the Spirit.

We need to realise that the blindness we have can be tempered by the opening of our inner eyes, to see and know that our God is actually at work.

Today, take a moment to realise that your moment of pain, or fear or lostness—all you are experiencing right now—is a set up from God for Him to bring about an incredible victory. God is leading you along paths that you've never walked on before. Allow Him to guide you and you'll soon experience the second half of the verse . . .

*' . . . I will turn the darkness into light before them
and make the rough places smooth. These are
the things I will do; I will not forsake them.'*
ISAIAH 42:16

He led Abraham along a path that he'd never walked down before, to a place he'd never been before. He led Moses into the desert for forty years, then led him out to be the deliverer of God's people.

He led Jacob into the wilderness for twenty years, then led him out to establish the nation of Israel. He led Joseph into slavery for thirteen years and then led him to be the guardian of the Hebrew people. He led David into the desert for eight years, while being hunted down by King Saul. He then led him out to be king over Hebron for seven years, then king over the whole of Israel.

Each one was led blind, yet their darkness was turned into light by the Hand of God. And it's the same with you.

Father,
Open the eyes of our hearts that we might know you better and see you more clearly. Help me see how strong and committed you are whilst everything looks to be falling apart. Help me to see that your 'glorious inheritance' for me isn't just eternity, but also you're stamping your authority upon this earth for me. Help me to believe in your incomparable power towards me.
In Jesus' name, Amen.

DECLARATION FORTY

I CHOOSE TO STEP ON IT!

> '... *Sit at my right hand until I make your*
> *enemies a footstool for your feet.*'
> **PSALM 110:1**

Have you ever found yourself in the situation where it feels like you are surrounded by enemies? Not so much the 'haters' but the everyday enemies of life—things like: busyness, financial restraint, relationship breakdown, loneliness, grief, pain, lack of sleep, ill health, a sense it is all out of control and a deep feeling that God is not moving anything at any point.

It's time to make footstools of those enemies. A footstool is something you stand on to reach for something that was previously out of reach.

Your current situation, the thing you see as your enemy, is about to become your footstool.

The grief you are experiencing may actually become your servant. It might actually become your footstool and lift you to new heights.

You don't need a ladder up, you need a footstool—a step up and on to the back of what you thought would break you. God is using your present surroundings to teach you to use them as a footstool to reach the things that had previously seemed unattainable.

> '*The Lord will extend your mighty sceptre from*
> *Zion, saying, "Rule in the midst of your enemies!"*'
> **PSALM 110:2**

This is the day for deliberately stepping up on the footstool of impossibility and realising that what the enemy meant for evil, God intended for your good—to reach the unreachable, to be propelled into the next thing, the next you and the next slice of your God-given inheritance.

> *Father,*
> *Help us to realise that in this very moment a platform and a way forward is actually in plain view. It is masqueraded as a problem and as an impasse, yet all the while, it is actually my future footstool. Help me to be brave, have the faith to look up, and possess the faith to step up. Create within me an emboldened spirit that reaches to the previously unreachable.*
> *In Jesus' name, Amen.*

DECLARATION FORTY-ONE

GENERATIONS UNITE!

'At that time Mary got ready and hurried to a town in the hill
country of Judea, where she entered Zechariah's home and
greeted Elizabeth. When Elizabeth heard Mary's greeting, the
baby leaped in her womb, and Elizabeth was filled with the
Holy Spirit. In a loud voice she exclaimed: "Blessed are you
among women, and blessed is the child you will bear! But why
am I so favoured, that the mother of my Lord should come to
me? As soon as the sound of your greeting reached my ears,
the baby in my womb leaped for joy. Blessed is she who has
believed that the Lord would fulfil His promises to her!"'
LUKE 1:39-45

Elizabeth was old. Mary was young. Yet when they met together something powerful happened in their midst.

Elizabeth should have been cynical, jealous, and petty towards Mary as she was notably old and had struggled all her life to get to that place of pregnancy. Here was the young whipper snapper, pregnant with ease. Yet she embraced her with all of her heart.

It's like the older generation and the younger generation coming together and seeing God explode in their togetherness. Maybe that's the key to God removing your fears and anxieties, and being filled again with all of the power of the Holy Spirit. It's found in the power of togetherness gently eroding all of your fears and phobias.

When we are young, our fear is often in missing out—we need to cling to the latest fashion, the latest fad and the latest in-crowd.

When we are middle-aged, our fear is often the loss of our youth and because our society idolises youth so much, we fear invisibility and rejection.

When we are older, our fear is often irrelevance, so we stop being the best version of ourself and revert to 'whatever will be will be!'

God wants to replace fear with a deep peace in our soul. His plan is to bring down the walls between the generations tearing down the arrogance of youth as well as the cynicism and rejection of the older years. Look at what happened in our story of Mary and Elizabeth. It may be time to remove the generational gap, across the generations and watch God touch your heart and soul. Only then, will something of the future leap within us by the power of the Spirit.

Father,
I now realise that my isolation is my undoing. Place people upon my heart today from across the generations so that my fears can dissipate and your love can be formed within me. Let me see this extraordinary union of Mary and Elizabeth and allow the truth of it to enter into my Spirit.
In Jesus' name, Amen.

DECLARATION FORTY-TWO

THE MIRACLE IS IN THE ORDINARY

'Jesus found a young donkey and sat on it, as it is
written; "Do not be afraid, Daughter of Zion; see
your king is coming seated on a donkey's colt."'
JOHN 12:14-15

All the fanfare was laid out for the exciting triumphal entrance of Jesus, yet He chose not to come to town on a white stallion but an ordinary donkey!

His purpose was outworked on the back of the unexpected. His purpose was outworked on the back of the unassuming. His purpose was outworked on the back of the little, rather than the large.

The purpose of God was carried along not by shouting, not in a blaze of glory, but quietly and slowly.

Sometimes we look for God in the planets aligning and we overlook the donkey. We overlook the signs and wonders within our normal day and get distracted by a search for the sensational. We sometimes dismiss smallness as inconsequence and miss the essence and direction that God wants to take us in.

Even today, God is outworking His covenant and His purpose for you in the little unassuming things that eventually combine to house the big.

To create wine, God used ordinary water in ordinary clay jars. When Samson slew the Phillistines, he used the jawbone of a donkey. When

David defeated Goliath, he used five smooth stones. When Jesus fed the five thousand, He used a little boy's lunch.

When Jesus launched His Church, He used a simple fisherman called Simon. When God fed Elijah, he used the Ravens, and when the widow at Zarephath came to Elijah, she came with a handful of flour yet left with a jar of flour that never ran out.

Faith is never anything more than a mustard seed. Prayer is nothing more than human words colliding with a divine God. He takes the little and makes it great.

Father,
Help me not to be dazzled by all of the talk of incredible moves of the Spirit and spectacular miracles. Help me to see that you use ordinary things to create extraordinary outcomes. Help me to see the donkey that will take me to my future.
In Jesus' name, Amen.

3

GOD IS POISED

'For I will pour water on the thirsty land,
and streams on the dry ground . . . '
ISAIAH 44:3

The wilderness always bears fruit, eventually. God specialises in finding people and recommissioning them in the desert. That's where God met Moses. He was in the back of the beyond but not out of sight from God. God took him from a wandering shepherd to a national deliverer in a place of dryness and isolation.

And it's the same for you. Your valley, your desert and your wilderness are the places that God does His best work. Let today be the beginning of your recommissioning and re-emergence. God is poised for the 'much-more' in your life.

DECLARATION FORTY-THREE

GOD HAS A GENTLE WHISPER

'Elijah was afraid and ran for his life. When he came to Beersheba in Judah, he left his servant there, while he himself went a day's journey into the wilderness. He came to a broom bush, sat down under it and prayed that he might die. "I have had enough, Lord," he said. "Take my life; I am no better than my ancestors." Then he lay down under the bush and fell asleep. All at once an angel touched him and said, "Get up and eat." He looked around, and there by his head was some bread baked over hot coals, and a jar of water. He ate and drank and then lay down again. The angel of the Lord came back a second time and touched him and said, "Get up and eat, for the journey is too much for you." So he got up and ate and drank. Strengthened by that food, he travelled forty days and forty nights until he reached Horeb, the mountain of God.'

1 KINGS 19:3-8

Have you ever come to the place in life where you have just had enough?

We think that when we get to this place, the way we feel is completely unique to us and that no one else has ever gone this way before. Yet it's not true. Elijah has been before all of us.

He had been out doing his day job of slaying the prophets of Baal, but was struck with fear. He got threatened by a woman, Jezebel, and found himself running away and hiding.

We have been known to condemn Elijah for his lack of courage but he was only running because he was at the end of himself—his day job had zapped him of all his strength. There is no condemnation from God for this, just encouragement and provision.

He didn't sheer off at that point—the scripture says he found strength in God's provision and then travelled forty days until he confronted his real challenge. Up until that point, he had only ever seen God in the spectacular. This time, God had chosen to present Himself not in a raging fire or a rumbling earthquake but in a still small voice. God has a 'gentle whisper' for you. It's time to take off your superman or superwoman outfit, get revived by some food, friends and fresh air and see that God hasn't left you. He's never been closer than He is right now.

God's kindness is also found in the way He delivers us. It's not always by the slaying of giants and the opening of the seas.

'But now, this is what the Lord says—He who created you, Jacob,
He who formed you, Israel: Do not fear, for I have redeemed you;
I have summoned you by name; you are mine. When you pass
through the waters, I will be with you; and when you pass through
the rivers, they will not sweep over you. When you walk through
the fire, you will not be burned; the flames will not set you ablaze.'
ISAIAH 43:1-2

God promises full deliverance but in His way, His strength and His timing.

Father,
Thank you for helping me realise again that I'm not you. Help me to
see that you love my humanness and you are ready now to take care of
my exhaustion and emptiness. Allow me to see you again in the stillness
and stormy-ness of my everyday.
In Jesus' name, Amen.

DECLARATION FORTY-FOUR

THE SHADE IS NOT WHERE I DWELL

> ' . . . to those who carry out plans that are not mine, forming an
> alliance, but not by my Spirit, heaping sin upon sin; who go down
> to Egypt without consulting me; who look for help to Pharaoh's
> protection, to Egypt's shade for refuge.'
>
> **ISAIAH 30:1-2**

The shade of Egypt represents Pharoah's protection. It speaks of yesterday's anointing. We are often afraid to step out of Pharaoh's shade so we make alliances, attitudes and decisions that keep us bound to Egypt. Yet it's the wrong place for us. It's our yesterday, not our tomorrow.

Our role is to introduce ourselves to newness—to be a prophetic doorway and to step out from under the umbrella of yesterday's protection. Your tomorrow is only as big as the decision you make today.

Shade, however comforting it is or has been, is not the place we are meant to dwell.

Sometimes our shade is the shade of comparison. We spend too much time in the shade of other people's identity and brilliance that we lose ourselves in it all. We let our own identity and creativity get shaded through comparison with theirs.

Sometimes our shade is the glory of our past. We've all had great seasons as well as moves of the Spirit that have meant so much to us. Even the times we were a child or a teenager, or the times our kids were still young or still at home have been streaked with so much glory that we have found it hard to move out from that shade into the sunshine of the new season.

Sometimes our shade is in respectability. We so want to be respected that we stop stepping out in case we fail again and end up with egg on our face.

Sometimes our shade is found in the familiarity of the last season of our lives. Sometimes we need to hear 'our beloved' speaking a fresh word into our hearts.

> *'My beloved spoke and said to me, 'Arise, my darling, my beautiful one, come with me. See! The winter is past; the rains are over and gone. Flowers appear on the earth; the season of singing has come, the cooing of doves is heard in our land. The fig-tree forms its early fruit; the blossoming vines spread their fragrance. Arise, come, my darling; my beautiful one, come with me.'*
> **SONG OF SONGS 2:10-13**

Let's rise up today and step out from whatever has been shading us. Let's take a hold of all that Christ has taken a hold of for us.

Father,
Today is a breakthrough day for me. A day when you will come by your Spirit and give me the ability to step through the doorway into my future purposes and calling. Give me the strength to come out of the shade and to step out in faith and courage into all you have for me. Give me a bigger understanding of my unique distinctives so that I can value once again the part I play in the awesome advancement of your Kingdom.
In Jesus' name, Amen.

DECLARATION FORTY-FIVE

I HAVE AN AUDIENCE OF ONE

'The angel of the Lord came and sat down under the oak in Ophrah that belonged to Joash the Abiezrite, where his son Gideon was threshing wheat in a winepress to keep it from the Midianites.'

JUDGES 6:11

So often we think of Gideon hiding away threshing wheat as some poor guy shaking in his boots, living in defeat and resignation.

But Gideon was doing what he knew to do, under severe threat from the Midianites.

He was hidden, but he was still producing and that's why the angel of the Lord came and sat down so close to him. God's spirit sits down, has time for and celebrates those who maintain diligence without an audience.

God has great respect and time for those who endure in obscurity, for those who choose to do what they can do while no one's watching and while no one really cares.

David's mighty victory came not on the battlefield while fighting Goliath, it came on the windswept hills protecting his father's sheep from advancing predators and unseen dangers. He killed a lion and a bear in the place of obscurity.

David's mighty men followed in his footsteps. One of his mighty men stood his ground to protect a field of lentils that wasn't his. He treated the field of lentils like a field of gold and won a great victory. He took a field of obscurity and owned it with all of his heart.

Elisha was found faithfully ploughing his fields with his oxen before he heard the call of God to receive the mantle of the prophet Elijah. Even Jesus served thirty faithful years learning to be a carpenter before he set off in His ministry that changed the world.

God is drawn to your faithfulness while no one is looking and no one seems to care.

Father,
Help me to maintain my energy and my integrity—not to look good in front of the masses, but to please my God and my Lord. Help me to be the best version of me, even when anxiety and fear, rejection and loss make me want to cave in and quit. Help me to remember that you're a faithful God full of kindness, thoughtfulness and love. In Jesus' name, Amen.

DECLARATION FORTY-SIX

IT ALL BEGINS HERE

> *'When the angel of the Lord appeared to Gideon, he said, "The*
> *Lord is with you, mighty warrior."'*
> **JUDGES 6:12**

When God sat down beside Gideon, He did not start with a grand pronouncement about Gideon's future, but instead He began with an affirmation of who he was.

God even did this to His own Son. When Jesus was being baptised, the Father declared,

> *'You are my beloved Son, with you I am well pleased.'*
> **MARK 1:11**

God affirms who you are in His eyes before you step out into an audience bigger than the audience of One.

Before you go to do anything great for God, He affirms you so you know that all the mighty battles you will win are not what captures His heart. Your works are not His currency, your understanding of sonship is!

> *'The seventy-two returned with joy and said, "Lord,*
> *even the demons submit to us in your name." He*
> *replied, "I saw Satan fall like lightning from heaven.*
> *I have given you authority to trample on snakes*
> *and scorpions and to overcome all the power of the*
> *enemy; nothing will harm you. However, do not*

rejoice that the spirits submit to you, but rejoice
that your names are written in heaven."'

LUKE 10:17-20

Sometimes we get caught up in all of the wrong things. We think that God's love language is performance, when His actual love language is relationship.

> *Father,*
> *Let me see that your love language to me is not the love language of success, scores on the board or in personal achievement, but in relationship with me as a person. Help me to rest in your arms of love and to know a love that resides upon me both in success and failure. I want you to touch my heart before you extend my hands. In Jesus' name, Amen.*

DECLARATION FORTY-SEVEN

GOD'S FRIENDSHIP IS MY REFUGE

'... It is more blessed to give than to receive.'
ACTS 20:35

Much can be achieved with the power of a great friendship. The only way to have a friend is to be one. Friendship requires friendliness, and friendliness requires not just a smile and a word of encouragement but also a willingness to become a little more vulnerable and a little less self-reliant.

Friendship is something to be given away, not grabbed a hold of. The moment you try to possess it and control it, it begins to die immediately.

Friendship should not firstly be a need. Friendship should be a freely given gift. To do that, you need to be feeding on your friendship with Heaven—Jesus loves us more than we love Him, which allows us to love others more than they love us. True friendship involves looking out for the needs of another often at the expense of ourselves.

Proverbs tell us that 'a friend loves at all times.' (Proverbs 17:17)

It's often interpreted that you must always be there as a friend. That's true, but here are three other aspects of friendship that often get missed.

Firstly, a friend always talks well of their friend. They don't offer behind the scenes information. They may say the truth to them, but always remain positive about their future and their potential. They never lose faith and belief.

Secondly, a good friend can either be a friend for life or a friend for a particular season. It's OK for friendship to change. And thirdly, the 'wounds from a friend can be trusted.' (Proverbs 27:6) Real friendship understands weakness and insecurities but doesn't excuse the damaging effects of them upon others. Real friendship encourages growth in the other person. 'There is a friend that sticks closer than a brother.' (Proverbs 18:24)

Friendship with God is a refuge. It's a place where you are totally understood and a place where you can hide under the shadow of His wings. Total security in that friendship enables us to be a friend. It's through His forgiveness that we can forgive and through His faithfulness we can be faithful.

Father,
Help me firstly to open again the gates of our friendship. Help me to be more vulnerable, more honest, more believing and more trusting in you. Help me to be a great receiver of your love and your grace and then help me to pour it all over my friendships and acquaintances. Free me from the knee-jerk reaction of jealousy and rejection by being committed to loving others more than they love me.
In Jesus' name, Amen.

DECLARATION FORTY-EIGHT

HIS ANOINTING STRENTHENS ME

*'So Jacob called the place Peniel, saying, "It is because I saw
God face to face, and yet my life was spared." The sun rose
above him as he passed Peniel, and he was limping because
of his hip. Therefore to this day the Israelites do not eat the
tendon attached to the socket of the hip, because the socket of
Jacob's hip was touched near the tendon.'*

GENESIS 32:30-32

This 'game' we are in as Christians is not about taking part. It's about winning. We've got to play this game to win.

In a boxing match, if you just stand there defensively, you'll lose. You'll lose simply because you showed no aggression and no strategy to advance.

We are called as Christians to get our gloves on, face the music and go for it.

Jacob, like many of us, struggled with life and struggled with God. It even left him with a limp.

We want so desperately to have that 'eye of the tiger' spirit or that 'knockout mentality' but we look in the mirror and see our greatest liability—ourselves. We're disappointed with what we see.

The good news is that God specialises in turning liabilities into assets and weaknesses into strengths.

Our 'limp' is not our limitation. In actual fact, it's our testimony to what God has brought us through.

We all have 'stuff' in our lives which seems to be left over from our past. For many of us it's rejection, insecurity, shyness and a lack of real confidence. Human weakness provides the ideal opportunity for the display of divine power. With God's power on it, it can become the area of our greatest strength. This is called 'the anointing.'

What weaknesses do you have that you can ask God to turn into strength? Where will His anointing take you today?

This is what Paul declared:

'Three times I pleaded with the Lord to take it away from me. But He said to me, 'My grace is sufficient for you, for my power is made perfect in weakness.' Therefore I will boast all the more gladly about my weaknesses, so that Christ's power may rest on me. That is why, for Christ's sake, I delight in weaknesses, in insults, in hardships, in persecutions, in difficulties. For when I am weak, then I am strong.'
2 CORINTHIANS 12:8-10

For when you are weak, His anointing makes you strong.

Father,
In you only, I am a warrior, a fighter, a boxer, a wrestler and a soldier. I'm here to fight the good fight of faith and to run the good race of destiny. I know that some battles you fight alone, but many you call us to fight with you with our weapons of the Word of God, the power of the Spirit, prophecy, prayer, faith, worship and straight out obedience and surrender to our God. Help me now to be covered in your anointing and use all of these weapons at my disposal.
In Jesus' name, Amen.

DECLARATION FORTY-NINE

I AM HIGHLY FAVOURED

*'Blessed are those who dwell in your house; they are
ever praising you. Blessed are those whose strength
is in you, whose hearts are set on pilgrimage.'*
PSALM 84:4-5

Blessed means to be highly favoured or to be greatly envied. God wants us to be people who live such amazing lives, it creates a longing in others to have what we're having. Your mandate is to stand out from the crowd.

We are all called to be envied. Not because of our talents or appearance but because of the Jesus in us and the blessing of God on us. Let's be people who wear God well, where grace and greatness collide.

There are many things we set our hearts on. We all have friends who have set their hearts on settling down. Some have set their hearts on riches, others on a future partner, a fabulous miracle or a real need for healing.

We are blessed when we set our hearts on the exciting journey of following after God.

God can't bless settlers and He can't bless those who worship His hand and not His heart. We need to be people who push out the boundaries of normal. Our lives should be characterised by movement. It takes risk to bloom.

God is calling us to be people who live magnificent lives with grace and greatness. People who push the boundaries of life and who refuse to be hemmed in. Let's go somewhere we've never been before!

It's time to realise just how blessed we are and walk in it. It's time to reset our hearts on pilgrimage and see our valleys turn to springs and pools, and our lives go from strength to strength.

Father,
I realise that this is my time to uproot, dig out my tent pegs and return to the great adventure of following hard after you. I choose today to come back into faith, to live life large and to break all boundaries of comfort and fear. I want to be envied for my joy, my generosity, my smile, my endurance, my blessings and my composure. I want to come back into actually changing my world and seeing your Kingdom come and will be done again in my life.
In Jesus' name, Amen.

DECLARATION FIFTY

THE BOUNDARIES ARE A BLESSING

'The boundary lines have fallen for me in pleasant places; surely I have a delightful inheritance.'
PSALM 16:6

My mum used to say to me, 'one day you will thank me for disciplining you.' I used to think it was a very strong thing to say. Now I realise how true it was.

Boundaries are channels of blessing. Floods of genius as well as brokenness come pouring down through our lives. With no boundaries, genius dissipates and brokenness remain broken.

'No discipline seems pleasant at the time, but painful. Later on, however, it produces a harvest of righteousness and peace for those who have been trained by it.'
HEBREWS 12:11

God is not a disciplinarian though. He is a Father who sees for us a better day, a stronger day and a bigger future.

If you take the tracks away from the train to give it freedom to go wherever it wants, you'll find it stuck in the dirt going nowhere. Its freedom is dependant upon its tracks. And it's the same for you. Your freedom and the long term blessing of it always requires boundaries. A boundary-less world is always full of fear, insecurity, depression and anxiety.

Observe a child who has been allowed to have anything they want at any time, and you'll see a deeply unhappy child.

Love and discipline are like a river and its banks. One without the other loses the power and purpose of both.

If you can interpret frustration, annoyances, persecutions, trials and simply not getting what you want when you want it as the Father's discipline, you immediately line your life up for a harvest of grace and peace. And who wouldn't want that?

Father,

I'm a little annoyed by all of this but I know that you're only disciplining me to take me higher and lead me further. You're wanting me to meet with your love and power so that my capacity and revelation can be enlarged—only because you have an enlarged territory for me to inherit. I understand that you are simply getting me ready for it. Give me great patience in the process.

In Jesus' name, Amen.

DECLARATION FIFTY-ONE

I AM A HOLY CREATION

*'They exchanged the truth about God for a lie,
and worshipped and served created things rather
than the Creator— who is forever praised.'*
ROMANS 1:25

We live in a world that is preoccupied with self-image and appearance. Selfies rarely reveal the true look of a person. Our society's self-obsession is slowly causing an inner self-destruction, where our insecurities are folding into life-controlling issues such as anorexia and self-harm.

Our bodies were not designed to be worshipped, they were designed to be utilised.

When we analyse society and its projection of the physical form, it seems to promote very little middle ground. There's very little balance in the whole thing. Our world promotes either superiority or rejection. We either feel amazing about how perfectly formed we are or we are squashed in insecurities about how ugly we are.

Both camps are not designed by God. God's viewpoint is actually in the middle. God wants us to live a balanced life—a balanced life in terms of what can we change and what can't we change, what's OK to touch and what shouldn't be touched!

What can we change? It is good to be a disciplined person, not in an obsessive way but in a constructive way. It gives you great guidelines. It's good to be disciplined, by caring for your body's fitness and health.

*'Do you not know that your bodies are temples of the
Holy Spirit, who is in you, whom you have received
from God? You are not your own; you were bought at a
price. Therefore honour God with your bodies.'*

1 CORINTHIANS 6:19-20

What can't we change? There are some things about ourselves that need to not only be accepted but celebrated.

I'm not totally against plastic surgery but the dangers of it far outweigh its successes. The moment you get a better shaped nose, you become discontent with the shape of your mouth. The moment you plump that up, you're discontented by the shape of your backside. It becomes a downward slope into discontentment, and discontentment breeds self-obsession. There's a point that you need to count your quirks as a part of you!

What shouldn't we touch? Your personality is a gift from God. Imagine noisy people trying to be quiet people. Imagine outdoorsy people trying to be indoorsy. Imagine melancholic people trying to be party animals!

We are all custodians of a unique history, a unique call from God, a unique personality and a unique love language that sets us apart from everyone else. If you see this as divine, you're on your way to absorbing both the acceptance and the celebration of the Father who deeply loves you.

Father,
Reduce my anxiety over my body image! I lay down my obsession at the altar of your grace and power. I lay down my self-hates, dissatisfaction and rejection with what I look like. Help me to accept what I cannot change and should not change. Thank you for making me in your image. In Jesus' name, Amen.

DECLARATION FIFTY-TWO

I AM HEALTHY FROM THE INSIDE OUT

'Dear friend, I pray that you may enjoy good health and that all may go well with you, just as you are progressing spiritually.'
3 JOHN 1:2

The world believes that health and prosperity start from the outside, yet the Word of God tells us that it actually starts from deep inside. Paul's prayers for the Ephesian church were all to do with the inner eyes of our hearts being opened, and our inner man being strengthened.

It's not what you've got that determines where you go in life, but it's who you are. He wants to strengthen our spirit first, then our soul and then our body. He wants to create in you a healthy mind, before he creates a healthy body.

What your eyes see and ears hear determine a lot about the health of your mind. Some of us need to stay away from the scales, some need to stay away from the magazines and some, from certain people on social media. You know where your trigger points are and you need to respect them and not allow yourself to be so easily led into temptation.

He also wants to create a healthy soul before a healthy body.

Health needs a good sense of humour—an ability to laugh at ourselves in order to depressurize and recalibrate. It's good to know what suits you and not to be a slave to fashion. The key is knowing you are loved just as you are—by both your closest friends and your amazing God.

Finally, God wants to create a healthy body.

A healthy body is one that carries us into old age. Our energy affects our attitude which affects our altitude. We need to pray for miracles, along side doing all we can to nourish our bodies with balanced food and exercise.

'For you created my inmost being; you knit me together in my mother's womb. I praise you because I am fearfully and wonderfully made; your works are wonderful, I know that full well.'

PSALM 139:13-14

Looking after ourselves may appear to slow us down, but it's all part of creating a long, sustainable future for the Will of God to prosper within our hands.

Father,
Thank you for creating me the way I am, even though I don't appreciate it every day. Help me to see what you see when you look at me. I lay down my anxiety and preoccupation with the way I look, and I resolve to live a healthy, happy life—the way you intended me to.
In Jesus' name, Amen.

DECLARATION FIFTY-THREE

I'M TAKING UP RESIDENCE

'Then David knew that the Lord had established
him as king over Israel and had exalted his
Kingdom for the sake of his people Israel.'
2 SAMUEL 5:12

Your hard times have a purpose. The potter is moulding your capacity and your motivation. David had a deep understanding in his heart that it was God who had established him as king and not just the approval of the people—he had this knowledge because he had faced adversity.

David had not had an easy journey to becoming king—he was the last one chosen amongst his peers; he faced a giant with five small stones; he was the subject of an unfair jealousy campaign; he was chased after, fearing for his life for almost a decade. He then waited in Hebron for seven years before he became king over all of Israel.

Adversity had shaped David not only to shoulder greatness but to also create a largeness of heart. Greatness is important to God as it means you have the power to lift people to another level. Adversity shapes us to handle greatness for the purpose for which it was intended.

'David then took up residence in the fortress
and called it the City of David ... '
2 SAMUEL 5:9

David chose to take up residence as he realised God had called him to greatness. You are in the right place, at the right time, doing the right thing. Choose to drop the fears, the anxieties and the false humility, and step into the greatness that God is calling you to. It's time to take up your residency.

> *Father,*
> *This is my moment of realisation. God give me the grace, energy, encouragement and vitality to live out the call and purpose of each day. I may not have what I need to be great tomorrow, but I have all I need to be great today. Thank you for arming me with strength for today as well as enlarging my capacity for tomorrow and empowering me for greatness. Thank you for the new confidence you are giving me to take up residency, like David, in my call and my purpose.*
> *In Jesus' name, Amen.*

DECLARATION FIFTY-FOUR

YOUR LOVE FOR ME IS LAVISH

'For it is God who works in you to will and to
act in order to fulfil His good purpose.'
PHILIPPIANS 2:13

Your Father God has a lavish love for you. Your future is embraced and encased by a lavish love. He lavishly bookends your past, your present moment and your future.

To be propelled into our tomorrow, God is at work deep below the surface of our lives, like a tide beneath the ocean. It is this lavish oceanic love that secures and anchors everything in our worlds, no matter what circumstance or season we find ourselves in.

Somehow, we have to know and trust that God sees our present moment in order for God to propel us into His future place. When Hagar was persecuted and ran away, her eyes were opened and she declared, "You are the God who sees me". It propelled Hagar into her potential. He sees where you are right now and still has one eye on your future.

In the story of The Woman at the Well in John 4, Jesus saw a woman in what was a seemingly insignificant and embarrassing moment—with a string of failed marriages and living with a man who was not her husband. He sees you in your 'hidden' place. He sees you in your moment. Yet, hidden does not mean forgotten.

Sometimes we feel like we are going round and round in circles, repeating history and living a life we never chose to live, like the crippled man at the pool of Bethesda. It can seem like someone else always gets the breakthrough before you.

But soon as the man began to pick up his mat, his legs were strengthed and he stepped into his future. As soon as he moved he was cured. It is often inactivity that paralyses us.

God doesn't tell us, however, to get running. He tells us to get walking! To run ahead is to put ourselves in danger and to lag behind is to give up and live in the past. To pick up your mat of yesterday and move into the stronger tomorrow is all that God requires.

Father,
I call this a lavish love. When all of the world is caught by their past, you're telling me to roll it up and walk. Thank you for the power of the cross that enables me to do this. Thank you for your ability to move me forward as I follow after you.
In Jesus' name, Amen.

DECLARATION FIFTY-FIVE

IT'S A NEW SEASON

*'Grain must be ground to make bread; so one
does not go on threshing it forever.'*
ISAIAH 28:28

How often do we find ourselves chipping away at the same old rock? We sometimes don't realise that we are living and working in an old season. Perhaps today it's time to do something different. It's time for change. It's time to stop threshing the same old grain.

It's time to let go of the old ways that are no longer propelling you forward. It's time to let go of 'analysis paralysis' that keeps your mind on the fruitlessness of the past. It's time for our expectancy levels not to be measured by what we have seen but upon what we believe. It takes new wineskins to house new wine.

If we don't reinvent our hearts, our minds, our plans and our ways, we will be stuck where we currently are. What brought us from A to B will probably not take us from B to C, or from C to D.

Today is a day to move from threshing to grinding. It's a new season that requires new skills and new techniques. Let's not be so locked into the 'old' that we miss the 'new'. Let's not be scared to try the new thing.

The book of Ecclesiastes tells us:

*'There is a time for everything, and a season for every activity
under the heavens: a time to be born and a time to die, a time
to plant and a time to uproot, a time to kill and a time to heal, a*

time to tear down and a time to build, a time to weep and a time
to laugh, a time to mourn and a time to dance, a time to scatter
stones and a time to gather them, a time to embrace and a time to
refrain from embracing, a time to search and a time to give up, a
time to keep and a time to throw away, a time to tear and a time
to mend, a time to be silent and a time to speak, a time to love
and a time to hate, a time for war and a time for peace.'
ECCLESIASTES 3:1-8

To move with the time and seasons of God in our lives is the source
of both our current peace and our future prosperity.

Father,
I need wisdom to know when the seasons are changing. Help me to
know when I've ploughed enough, sown enough, watered enough and
harvested enough. Help me to know when to let something go and when
to pick something up. Help me to find my new wineskin and not get too
attached to the old ones.
In Jesus' name, Amen.

DECLARATION FIFTY-SIX

I AM NAMED BY GOD

'... He calls His own sheep by name and leads them out.'
JOHN 10:3

God does not call us as a group; He calls us as a person. This is not mass conscription—this is an individual invitation. You have an individual 'name' that is just yours. Your name represents your personality, God's plans and assignments for you, as well as your gifts and abilities. Your name is the new you created by His Spirit, your unique quirks as well as your secret desires and longings. He knows you, He calls you and leads you by name.

Trying to answer to your neighbour's name is like forging their signature on the roll call of Heaven. He has an individual plan for you and an individual solution for you.

In Genesis we learn about the two brothers Jacob and Esau. Esau, the oldest, was a skilful hunter—a man of the open country, while Jacob was a quiet man who stayed at home and was closely connected to his mother.

Esau was emotionally led and sold his birthright to his youngest brother for the bowl of stew. He let go of who he was. If he had realised the consequences of that decision he would never have let go of his birthright. You need to value the calling that God has uniquely placed upon your life and not allow the spirit of the world to ever trade with it.

You are priceless as well as matchless. Never sell yourself short. This is what the Lord says,

'. . . *I have summoned you by name; you are mine.*'
ISAIAH 43:1

This is not a matter of having a strong ego, this is about having a strong identity that comes from the breath of heaven.

Father,
Help me to hear my name when you call it. Thank you for knowing me and making me a new creation. I have chosen to go with the new and be out with the old. I anticipate fresh ways, fresh winds and fresh waves of your Spirit washing over me.
In Jesus' name, Amen.

DECLARATION FIFTY-SEVEN

HIS MEMORY IS FLAWLESS

'And the words of the Lord are flawless, like silver
purified in a crucible, like gold purified seven times.'
PSALM 12:6

God is always completely trustworthy and eternally flawless. He's a God who is with us at every stage in our lives. He's the one who knows everything about us. He's with us, and even in our mess His Word remains intact—complete, unbroken and unsoiled.

Through the storms, fears, triumphs, laughter and disappointments, He is with us through the whole of life's journey from start to end. He covers our seemingly endless ability to stuff up. Every time we fail He covers for us and continues to pursue everything He started in us. And it won't stop until He's completed all He has planned to do.

'As far as the east is from the west, so far has He
removed our transgressions from us.'
PSALM 103:12

Our sins are designed by His flawless Word to never meet us again. They're removed, taken away, disintegrated, extinguished, obliterated, annihilated and muted until there's absolutely nothing left at all. Not even a sniff in the air.

Though we often find it impossible to forget after we have forgiven, God's ways are different to ours. He has never kept a catalogue of wrongdoings to bring out as an arsenal on a bad day. Yet, His forgetfulness is limited only to our sin.

> '... *Though she may forget, I will not forget you!*
> *See, I have engraved you on the palms of my*
> *hands; your walls are ever before me.'*
> **ISAIAH 49:15-16**

Just as an engraved piece of jewellery is forever personal to you, you are engraved as a keepsake close to God's heart. He is forever reminded He has personal responsibility for you.

You can trust in God because even when you feel incredibly alone. You can know He remembers you always. His memory is flawless.

Father,
I thank you wholeheartedly for your gift of total and utter forgiveness, your present of sheer forgetfulness and your absolute treat of remembrance. Thank you for remembering me every second of every day by engraving me on the palm of your hand. You are so fabulous and so faithful. Help me to be the same.
In Jesus' name, Amen.

DECLARATION FIFTY-EIGHT

HIS WORDS ARE IN MY MOUTH

*'Set a guard over my mouth Lord, keep
watch over the door of my lips.'*
PSALM 141:3

Our words, like doorways, are things we can use to get to new destinations
and opportunities. They can also be like a trap door that can rob us
from ever stepping forward into our destiny.

*'The tongue has the power of life and death, and
those who love it will eat its fruit.'*
PROVERBS 18:21

Our mouths are like fountains that either create life and unity or
create death and destruction. Our responsibility is to monitor our
mouths to make sure they release love, kindness, encouragement and
faith whenever they're opened.

It is amazing how idle chatter forms destructive whispers that create
a culture which can be completely undesirable to faith and love. Jesus
always chose to cover His speech with grace rather than condemnation.

A unique body of believers who speak well of each other create a
powerful undivided church that is strong in both authority and anointing.
Today, let's be purposeful in the words we use and use them to uplift
and build people in our world.

When Jesus saw Simon he declared that he would be called Peter. Instead of seeing 'a reed' swayed by popular opinion he saw 'a rock', strong and steadfast in the face of opposition and aggression. Jesus used the power of words to prophesy God's purposes into human affairs.

The book of James tells us that our words are like the rudder of a huge ship, and like a small spark that sets on fire a great forest. The art of taming the tongue is essential in launching the right ships and setting the right fires that cause His will to powerfully unfold in our lives.

Father,
Help me to create a culture of faith through the words that I speak. Help me to create a culture of love through the words I share and a culture of hope and expectancy through the words that I choose. Help me to put your words in my mouth and build a future of life and abundance. In Jesus' name, Amen.

DECLARATION FIFTY-NINE

FAITH IS THE CURRENCY OF HEAVEN

'Jesus, turned and saw her. "Take heart, daughter," He said, "your faith has healed you." And the woman was healed at that moment.'
MATTHEW 9:22

God's Church, your ministry and all of your future is built upon nothing but unshakeable faith. Faith is the key. Let's take a moment to stoke up our faith.

Faith always bounces back and always expects; faith always believes that God will do what He says He will do; faith also knows that whatever your eyes and ears tell you, Jesus is still on the throne.

Faith is unaffected by changes to our circumstances and celebrates the new season before it actually appears. Faith wakes up each morning and wonders what miracles will happen that day as well as the next.

'. . . Truly I tell you, if you have faith as small as a mustard seed you could say to this mountain, "Move from here to there," and it will move. Nothing will be impossible for you.'
MATTHEW 17.20

Our problem is that we are always thinking that we need a lot of faith to move the mountains in our world. The truth is, we only need faith the size of a tiny seed. Often we don't need more faith, just less doubt. Because faith is so small it's easy to neglect it, forget about it, ignore it and lose it. We need to prize it because within it holds the key to our future breakthroughs.

A faith culture is created by those who always get up to fight another day. They know their God, they know His faithfulness and they know He comes through at just the right time. Although you may not know it, you have actually been rebuilding a culture of faith in your life. You've been relearning the power of speech, reigniting the necessity of His Word and restoring the need for total trust in God to create an environment of faith within which all of your future will grow.

> *Father,*
> *I know that faith is the currency of Heaven, so I choose to align myself with your Word, your promises and your Spirit in order to create my own faith environment in which your Kingdom can flourish.*
> *In Jesus' name, Amen.*

DECLARATION SIXTY

I LIVE BY FAITH

*'They are the kind who worm their way into homes and gain
control over gullible women, who are loaded down with
sins and swayed by all kinds of desires, always learning but
never able to come to a knowledge of the truth.'*
2 TIMOTHY 3:6-7

For faith to be real, it has to be able to confront reality, not escape from
it. Fairytale Christianity never acknowledges reality. Many operate in
this La-La Land because of deep-rooted insecurity. God always deals
with today's deficiencies and gives real hope—not false hope. God gives
tangible, understandable, go-do-it wisdom to those who seek after it.

We often say to ourselves, 'Let's just leave that 'too hard' basket
for another day', or 'Tomorrow, I'll lose weight', 'Later I'll work on my
issues' or 'Someday I'll find it in my heart to forgive'. The problem is,
tomorrow usually never comes.

Tomorrow doesn't deal with the realities that crowd you and surround
today. Today is our time for real personal responsibility. Focusing too
much on tomorrow denies the power of what we have in our hand today.

*'Do not withhold good from those to whom it is due, when it is your
power to act. Do not say to your neighbour, "Come back tomorrow
and I'll give it to you", when you already have it with you.'*
PROVERBS 3:27-28

Be aware of what is in your hand today and what has been given to you already by the hand of God. Don't be like the world that pretends it has nothing to give as a cover up for a lack of desire or a lack of responsibility. If you have it, it's time to put it to use.

It's our 'roll up our sleeves' time. It is said of the woman in Proverbs 31, 'She sets about her work vigorously.' Today, let's do the same.

Father,
I refuse to put off until tomorrow what I can do today. Help me to confront reality with my faith and not to avoid it. Allow me to grow in my maturity and responsibility and become more proactive than I've ever been. Take away all of my excuses to not do all I can do.
In Jesus' name, Amen.

DECLARATION SIXTY-ONE

MY DARK SIDE IS HIS OPPORTUNITY

'... I waited patiently for the Lord; He turned to me and heard my
cry. He lifted me out of the slimy pit, out of the mud and mire; He
set my feet on a rock and gave me a firm place to stand. He put a
new song in my mouth, a hymn of praise to our God. Many will
see and fear the Lord and put their trust in Him.'

PSALM 40:1-3

We all have a dark side; a deep weakness that hides itself deep within you.
Today be assured that there is purpose and power in it. The Bible talks
about how He anoints our weakness. It tells us how we are not meant to
boast as the world boasts, about our inherent strengths and self-made
successes, but to boast in the power of God resting on our humanity.

God's design is that He doesn't just touch our darker side, but makes
it a firm place and a platform for a kingly future. God wants us to bring
our inner self to Him so that He can heal it, wash it with His Word and
His presence and propel us into our future.

God's purpose for your life is that we lay before Him our hidden
self. He then transforms it into something so powerful that the world
stands up to take notice. Society does not want religiosity or hypocrisy.
It actually wants to see humanity swallowed up in victory; humanity
packaged in glory.

There is a dark side of the moon—and although it receives
approximately the same amount of light as the other side, the dark side

of the moon is the portion that always seems to face away from the sun. A telescope in Hawaii once revealed that the colour of the dark side is not grey or black, but is in reality a beautiful turquoise.

> *'Afflicted city, lashed by storms and not comforted, I will rebuild you with stones of turquoise, your foundations with lapis lazuli. I will make your battlements of rubies, your gates of sparkling jewels, and all your walls of precious stones. All your children will be taught by the Lord, and great will be their peace. In righteousness you will be established: Tyranny will be far from you; you will have nothing to fear. Terror will be far removed; it will not come near you. If anyone does attack you, it will not be my doing; whoever attacks you will surrender to you. "See, it is I who created the blacksmith who fans the coals into flame and forges a weapon fit for its work."'*
>
> **ISAIAH 54:11-16**

God's promise to you today is that your dark side will become your beautiful side—He doesn't need your strength today, He needs your weakness! He wants to be the strong one in your relationship.

Father,
I believe that all of my dark side is an opportunity for you to bring about such a change in me that one day I'll actually thank you for my flaws. I declare that each of my flaws are like windows of opportunity for the power of God to enter in, take control and cover with the precious stones of His glory.
In Jesus' name, Amen.

DECLARATION SIXTY-TWO

HE IS IN THE DISCOMFORT

'But the woman had taken the two men and hidden them
… She had taken them up to the roof and hidden them
under the stalks of flax she had laid out on the roof.'
JOSHUA 2:4-6

Rahab the prostitute was used greatly by God to hide Joshua's spies in Jericho to allow them to report back to him. These spies, at this point in the story, would definitely not be looking like world-conquering heroes—hidden under stalks of flax, on an exposed roof-top, in the home of a prostitute!

They didn't allow discomfort, however, to dislodge their dream. And nor should you. Sometimes discomfort is actually God's protection as the enemy of your destiny passes by. Don't abandon discomfort before it does its work.

Out of the depths of an uncomfortable situation, the true facts of what was happening were revealed to the spies.

'I know that the Lord has given you this land and that a
great fear of you has fallen on us, so that all who live in this
country are melting in fear because of you … When we
heard of it, our hearts melted in fear and everyone's courage
failed because of you, for the Lord your God is the God in
Heaven above and on the Earth below.'
JOSHUA 2:9-11

While these men were hiding, feeling small and unnoticed, the power of God was spreading across the plains and hills of Canaan. The spies may have been small, they may have been in the minority, and may have been unseen but the whole and trembled because God was on the move.

'So we fix our eyes not on what is seen, but on what is unseen, since what is seen is temporary, but what is unseen is eternal.'
2 CORINTHIANS 4:18

The spies didn't return saying how embarrassing and uncomfortable their experience had been—they came back and said, 'The Lord has surely given the whole land into our hands; all the people are melting in fear because of us.' (Joshua 2:24). They chose to speak out the unseen and to speak out a good report. Let's choose to do the same today, as we look beyond any discomfort we may be feeling and trust in a God who is always on the move and bringing about our success.

Father,
I know that between the promise and the promise coming to pass, I will experience some discomfort. I choose to pick up my cross and follow you, knowing that I will pass through this valley of the shadow of death into a place of glory and resurrection. Thank you that you are always working things together for my good, even when I can't see it.
In Jesus' name, Amen.

DECLARATION SIXTY-THREE

GOD IS NOT DISILLUSIONED WITH ME

'The Lord will guide you always; He will satisfy your needs in a sun scorched land and will strengthen your frame. You will be like a well-watered garden, like a spring whose waters never fail.'
ISAIAH 58:11

Sometimes we just need to remind ourselves that God is for us and that God is with us. Today, God also wants to remind us of who He is and what He's like. Have you ever been offered a role or a position and thought to yourself, 'if they really knew me, the real me, the warts and all me, there is no way they would trust me or offer me that place or position.'

We are totally known by God. He knows us through and through and that is actually a good thing. He says, 'I will cover this' and 'I will use that'. As I've already declared, He is the master in covering our weakness.

The wonderful thing about being totally known is that He doesn't think that we are dumb or inept or even silly in the anxieties and faults we have and carry. He doesn't think our fears are stupid. He knew that we would have them. Otherwise God would never have said, 'cast all your anxieties on me'. He knows that we were just human, and He prepared Himself for that.

God's plan was that you would become a highly functioning and significant person through His Spirit with an imperfect body and an imperfect heart.

'Record my misery; list my tears on your scroll—are they not in your record? Then my enemies will turn back when I call for help. By this I will know that God is for me.'

PSALM 56:8-9

He hears your voice, He lists your tears and He itemises your anxieties. He never belittles you or demeans you. He values you. Your concerns are His concerns. They are His priority.

'And the God of all grace, who called you to His eternal glory in Christ, after you have suffered a little while, will Himself restore you and make you strong firm and steadfast.'

1 PETER 5:10

He, Himself, personally restores you. This is not a selfhelp job; this a surrender job. He does the restoring, not you. Sure, your restoration involves your commitment, but most of all your surrender.

'To Him who is able to keep you from stumbling, and to present you before His glorious presence without fault and with great joy.'

JUDE 1:24

Though we lose our balance from time to time there is one who always stands next to you to prevent you from falling. He's committed to the very end.

Father,
I thank you that you know my inner working more than I know myself.
I thank you that you have already made arrangements to make me the
best version of me that I could ever be. I'm thankful that in all of my
mess you create a message that will impact generations.
In Jesus' name, Amen.

GOD IS MIGHTY

'Therefore God exalted Him to the highest place and gave Him the name that is above every name, that at the name of Jesus every knee should bow, in Heaven and on Earth and under the Earth, and every tongue acknowledge that Jesus Christ is Lord, to the glory of God the Father.'
PHILIPPIANS 2:9-11

God is in control. Everything on Earth is under His sovereign rule. He allows powers to rule and then orchestrates their fall. He allows free will and then limits it by His mighty hand. His might not only exists in the realm of His sovereignty, it's made available to a people of faith. You can't create the future, but you can miss it. By faith, we can access His victory and His triumph and possess all of the plans He's set aside for us.

Let's add to our faith prayers of faith, declarations of faith and steps of faith and watch His might gain prominence all over our worlds.

DECLARATION SIXTY-FOUR

I ABIDE IN HIM

'Whoever dwells in the shelter of the Most High will rest in the shadow of the Almighty. I will say of the Lord, "He is my refuge and my fortress, my God, in whom I trust. Surely He will save you from the fowler's snare and from the deadly pestilence. He will cover you with His feathers, and under His wings you will find refuge; His faithfulness will be your shield and rampart."

PSALM 91:1-4

This scripture is for the active, not the inactive. 'The fowler's snare' and 'deadly pestilence' are not found under your duvet, they're found in the hustle and bustle of those launching out on life's great adventure, seeing His kingdom come and His will be done.

The greatest of storms are found in the high seas, and the greatest diseases are found in the greatest concentrations of humanity. Because we're called to both, we need to know that God will protect us.

As we move on in our calling, God promises that He will be our refuge, fortress, shield and rampart. A rampart is the defensive wall of a city with a broad walkway on the top. He gives us a broad walkway and viewpoint over the plague and the pestilence and over the concerns of life that threaten our propulsion into His purposes.

'Dwelling in the shelter of the Most High' promises us shade from heat. The sun still glares down but there is a shadow that protects us. Dwelling in this shelter is a choice that involves stepping out into the unknown, conscious of the promise of God, and trusting in His protective faithfulness.

What great exploits stand in the future of a man or woman who chooses to trust God over taking life in their own hands. Plague and pestilence may be threatening, yet God's faithfulness protects.

So much so, you often are completely unaware of His many deliverances.

It's time to dwell in His shelter. It's time to rest in His shadow. It's time to see again that the battle belongs to the Lord. It's time to see again that our God holds us, protects us and covers us until our enemies are both disarmed and defeated.

Father,

Remind me today who you are. Remind me that you know me and remind me that you are committed to restoring me. Remind me that you have a future for me, remind me that you protect me and remind me that you are with me. Isaiah 41:10 says, 'So do not fear for I am with you; do not be dismayed for I am your God. I will strengthen you and help you; I will uphold you with my righteous right hand.' I take that as my promise and my peace as I continue throughout my day. I will dwell with you and allow you to dwell and abide in me. Thank you that if I abide in you and your Word in me, an open Heaven is formed over my world. I declare your favour upon my prayers and my decisions. In Jesus' name, Amen.

THIS IS MY 'EVEN THOUGH' MOMENT

*'He took him outside and said, "Look up at the sky
and count the stars—if indeed you can count them."
Then He said to him, "So shall your offspring be."'*
GENESIS 15:5

Everything starts with a promise. Within each of us is both a desire to achieve and do something amazing as well as a promise—a word or a whisper from God.

Abraham discovered, however, the promises of God involved two Christian swear words—patience and waiting. Patience and waiting sometimes feel like the two ugly stepsisters that are trying to stop Cinderella going to the ball.

In the busyness of life and the impatience of waiting, Abraham actually lost the plot and did something really stupid. He got sick of staring at the ugly sisters. And so Ishmael was conceived.

What was he thinking? What possessed him?

We could easily ask the same questions of our lives. 'What possessed me?'

'Why did I quit?'

'Why did I back down from the purposes of God?'

Even though Abraham had totally stuffed up and subverted the will of God in his life and even though he had gone completely off course—

God is the God of the 'Even Though'. Even though Abraham made a great mistake, God still wanted to use him.

Even though Abraham had an Ishmael, God still gave him an Isaac. Even though Jonah went the other way, God's Word came to him a second time (Jonah 3:1). Even though Sarah laughed at God's promise of a son, she still conceived and gave birth to him (Genesis 18:12).

It's the same with us. Our destinies are not aborted by our mistakes. God still wants to fulfil His promise to you. God is the God of the 'Even Though' in your life.

Today is your 'Even Though' moment—whether it's a major stuff up or simply allowing defeat and insecurity to smother your potential, God is ready and able to realign you back with His purpose.

Father,
I'm going to deny the lie that you have no place for the flawed. I'm declaring that my Ishmael may be distracting me, but my Isaac is on its way. I thank you that you specialise in those who have missed the mark and that you will not abandon the plans you have for me. I thank you that I'm back in your perfect will and your perfect timing.
In Jesus' name, Amen.

DECLARATION SIXTY-SIX

I ACCEPT THE CUP

'He withdrew about a stone's throw beyond them, knelt down and prayed, "Father, if you are willing, take this cup from me; yet not my will, but yours be done."'

LUKE 22:41-42

On this day, Jesus was at the end of Himself and asked God if He could take this unbearable cup of destiny away.

It is not wrong to call out to God about the weight of destiny—about the weight of the 'cup of calling' that you are carrying. It is absolutely normal. If you are feeling like you just can't carry on with the pressure today, you are not insane or ungodly—you are normal.

'An angel of Heaven appeared to Him and strengthened Him.'

LUKE 22:43

For some of us today, God himself wants to send His angel to strengthen us.

After this strengthening from Heaven, Jesus went from crying out for the cup to be taken from Him, to instructing His disciples to start praying so they wouldn't fall into temptation. He then proceeded to go back a second time and asked His Father again to take the cup from Him. The scripture also records Him going back a third time!

To struggle with destiny and life is not wrong. Even Jesus did it. He gets humanity. He moved from discouragement to lifting others in a heartbeat and still fulfilled His destiny. He went on from this place of 'defeat' and accomplished the greatest victory ever—the salvation of mankind. The Bible says He was without sin—so obviously a moment of 'tough' was not considered by God to be sinful. God considers your perceived failure today not as sin, but as a rung in the ladder of your greatest victory yet.

Father,
I am relieved! I thank you that my wrestle within does not disqualify me from leading my family, my business, my ministry and my church. I thank you that my humanity is only just that. Now allow divinity to enter into my humanity and give me a boldness and resolve to move on. In Jesus' name, Amen.

DECLARATION SIXTY-SEVEN

I AM SWALLOWED UP IN VICTORY

*'Then they took Jonah and threw him overboard, and the
raging sea grew calm. At this the men greatly feared the Lord,
and they offered a sacrifice to the Lord and made vows to
him. Now the Lord provided a huge fish to swallow Jonah . . .
From inside the fish, Jonah prayed to the Lord His God.'*
JONAH 1:15-17, 2:1

The story of Jonah is a powerful one: a runaway out on the high seas,
making every effort to distance himself from the 'hard' and from all
the stuff that he was scared of. He ended up being thrown out into
the ocean and rescued by a whale. Jonah's rescue involved him being
swallowed whole.

Your humanity is completely swallowed up as well—in victory. Jesus'
victory was where humanity met immortality. He rose in triumph for
your victory.

*'For the perishable must clothe itself with the imperishable, and
the mortal with immortality . . . then the saying that is written will
come true: "Death has been swallowed up in victory."'*
1 CORINTHIANS 15:53-54

Today is 'new clothing' day. We are going shopping today, not to be
condemned by our humanity but to embrace the victory won for us.

Today we have been swallowed whole. We have had a victory won for us—a provision for our mortality.

God's grace covers your weak moments and gives you courage for tomorrow. Our weakness just magnifies the power of the grace of God, and that power is the fuel in our jet packs that enables us to get up and go again.

The bedrock of this whole thing is that God loves us so unequivocally. He is so accepting, so encouraging and so celebrating of us. His love never fails and never gives up on us. His love never runs out. His love never stops. It's infinite, it's patient, it's believing—it's seamless in every way. It's never reassessed because of your perceived failure. He does not put restrictions on your acceptability. He just accepts, forgives and clothes your humanity in victory.

'That you may have power, together with all the Lord's holy people, to grasp how wide and long and high and deep is the love of Christ, and to know this love that surpasses knowledge—that you may be filled to the measure of all the fullness of God.'
EPHESIANS 3:18-19

May God grant you the power of the revelation that you are deeply loved—the 'immeasurably more' poured out, causing your weaknesses to be swallowed up in victory. His love is wide with amazing diversity, long with incredible patience, high with unmatched strength and deep with rich understanding and sympathy.

Father,
Help me to see that I'm not disqualified from your love and victory, but swallowed up and absorbed by it. Thank you that your love is not dependent upon my efforts but upon your nature. You simply cannot stop loving. Allow my faith to open the door to both see it and experience it. In Jesus' name, Amen.

DECLARATION SIXTY-EIGHT

I CHOOSE A PURE HEART

*'Who may ascend the mountain of the Lord? Who
may stand in His holy place? The one who has clean
hands and a pure heart, who does not trust in an idol
or swear by a false god. They will receive blessing from
the Lord and vindication from God their Saviour.'*
PSALM 24:3-5

This is how it works when you have kept your integrity, been faithful
and fostered a right spirit—you are promised blessing from the Lord!
It's not that these things earn you favour but they position you into the
place of favour.

It's easy to think that God can care more about our faith than about
our actions. If faith is the currency of Heaven then where is the need
for 'clean hands and a pure heart'? Yet, everything we do is evidence
of everything we believe or don't believe. A life of integrity is proof of
a life of trust and a life of faith. It displays to our God the depth of our
trust and our dependence upon Him.

*'May integrity and uprightness protect me,
because my hope, Lord, is in you.'*
PSALM 25:21

Your single hearted devotion to God is your protection against the
forces that rage against you and the temptations that try to sway you.

Integrity simply means wholeness. It means to be undivided, totally unified and single-minded. Often our hearts are divided by our affections to earthly things—we easily over-attach ourselves to people, possessions and places and find our heartstrings being pulled in all directions. At these times, we need to re-align ourselves with not what we want, but what we really really want for our lives. We need to dig deep through our emotions to find our true heart's desire that wants to love and be led by the true lover of our souls.

We need to refind the place of our first love—the place where God first touched us with His love and made us born again by His Spirit. Our integrity and our wholehearted devotion to God is then rekindled and our protection secured. Life becomes easier as we love one God, our God, with all of our hearts, minds and souls.

This takes humility, true repentance and restoration of your deep desire for Heaven itself. I know you want it.

Father,
Help me to add to my faith a new respect and honour for you and your
Word. Help me to no longer live with a divided heart. I choose today to
repent and turn back to you with all my heart. Give me an undivided
heart, a whole heart and a soft heart as I place my hope back into you
and align my thoughts and actions with your will. In Jesus' name, Amen.

DECLARATION SIXTY-NINE

IT'S TIME TO DIG DITCHES

'I will exalt you, my God the King; I will praise
your name for ever and ever.'
PSALMS 145:1

Do you feel today that there are areas of your life that are barren and dry?

King Jehoshaphat once cried out to the prophet Elisha as he found himself and his army in the middle of a desert on their way to war, with no more water left for his men or his animals. He felt they had been doing the right thing, yet they found themselves in a barren place.

This is what Elisha replied:

'And he said, "Thus says the Lord: 'Make this valley full of ditches.'
For thus says the Lord: 'You shall not see wind, nor shall you see
rain; yet that valley shall be filled with water, so that you, your cattle,
and your animals may drink.' And this is a simple matter in the
sight of the Lord; He will also deliver the Moabites into your hand.
Also, you shall attack every fortified city and every choice city, and
shall cut down every good tree, and stop up every spring of water,
and ruin every good piece of land with stones." Now it happened
in the morning, when the grain offering was offered, that suddenly
water came by way of Edom, and the land was filled with water.'
2 KINGS 3:16-20

When Jehoshaphat's men started to dig ditches in the dust, it started to rain in the highlands of Edom. It took until daybreak for the water to flow down from the hills and fall into the ditches. The water mixed with the clay in the soil and looked like blood, so when the enemy came down unarmed to see what had happened to Israel's army, their fate was sealed. Victory for Israel was assured.

It's time to start digging ditches in your desert:

Dig ditches of praise.

Dig ditches of faith.

Dig ditches of declaration.

Dig ditches of expectation.

Dig new ditches of obedience to your God.

For Jehoshaphat, it may have cut against all logic and made the men even more thirsty than they were before they started to dig, yet it was the masterstroke of their success. It's time to hear from 'the prophet' and do whatever He tells you. On the other side of your obedience lies the rain of victory.

> *Father,*
> *I know that you don't first respond to faith but to the proof of faith found in our actions and in our obedience. Today I say 'yes Lord' to living according to my true convictions, talking according to my true beliefs and thinking according to my true commitments before God. I now pick up my spade and start to dig my ditches in anticipation for both the refreshing rain of God and the inevitable victories that you will bring to my life and world.*
> *In Jesus' name, Amen.*

DECLARATION SEVENTY

I HAVE A DIVINE CONNECTION

'For just as each of us has one body with many
members, and these members do not all have the same
function, so in Christ we, though many, form one body,
and each member belongs to all the others.'
ROMANS 12:4-5

We've all known someone who achieved something not because of what they knew but because of who they knew. There are many things we can gain by knowing the right people by our connections, not by our competence. God has designed us with a need to be connected. Our success depends entirely on our connections.

Firstly, it depends upon our connection with Heaven.

"'. . . because the splendour I had given you made
your beauty perfect," declares the Sovereign Lord.'
EZEKIEL 16:14

God wants you first to be confident in who you are, not in what you do. Your sonship and daughterhood is a huge key to you being personally fulfilled. We need to know your connection with Heaven is what makes our beauty complete. His grace and our humanity create amazing wonder.

Secondly, it depends upon our connections as brothers and sisters.

'From Him the whole body, joined and held together
by every supporting ligament, grows and builds
itself up in love, as each part does its work.'
EPHESIANS 4:16

Each part needs each other. In the world, life is disjointed and disconnected, with so many living in loneliness and despair. God never wanted the church to look like that; He designed the church to be filled with the consistent love and commitment that comes from real brotherhood and real sisterhood.

Thirdly, it depends upon our connection to motherhood and fatherhood.

'I am reminded of your sincere faith, which first lived
in your grandmother Lois and in your mother Eunice
and, I am persuaded, now lives in you also.'
2 TIMOTHY 1:5

There are 'sons and daughters' and 'nieces and nephews' that need what you have right now. There are 'mothers and fathers' waiting for 'daughters and sons' to emerge so they can fully cover us and nurture us. The power of family creates an invaluable sharing of strengths and abilities. Our successes come from breaking the barriers of prejudice and isolation. It comes from us holding hands across age barriers, background barriers, race barriers, and all our secret barriers, that allows God to pour out blessings that cannot be contained.

Father,
Help me to come to the realisation that I have a need to connect in so many different ways. I rebuke the lie that I don't actually need anyone. I choose to both reach out today with a heart of encouragement and be reached out to by holding out a hand of vulnerability and humility. In Jesus' name, Amen.

DECLARATION SEVENTY-ONE

IT'S HARVEST TIME!

'Others, like seed sown on good soil, hear the word,
accept it, and produce a crop—some thirty, some sixty,
some a hundred times what was sown.'

MARK 4:20

The Word of God is never dormant.

It's active and powerful. Jesus used the analogy of God being like a farmer, the Word of God being like seed and the soil being like our hearts. As the farmer went to sow his seed some fell on hard soil where it simply bounced off and produced nothing. Some seed fell on shallow soil where it grew for a short time but was cut short by 'trouble and persecution'. Some seed fell on overcrowded soil where the worries of life and the deceitfulness of wealth caused it to wither. The majority of the seed fell on good soil and produced a crop magnificently larger than anything that was sown.

Even while some seed has been both stolen and thwarted in your world, a secret harvest has been slowly growing. Night and day, in season and out of season, the seed of God's Word has been secretly growing within the soil of our hearts.

All by itself it will produce a harvest—at first just a glimmer, then eventually an overflow up to one hundred times that which was sown.

It will seem like it's almost overnight. A harvest will suddenly burst forth—a harvest of salvation, a harvest of success and a harvest of righteousness. Never be discouraged, however, by the sight of a brown field. It may look like nothing is actually happening but don't be fooled. Continue to believe and never give up.

'Trust in the Lord and do good; dwell in the land and enjoy safe pasture. Take delight in the Lord, and He will give you the desires of your heart. Commit your way to the Lord; trust in Him and He will do this: He will make your righteous reward shine like the dawn, your vindication like the noonday sun. Be still before the Lord and wait patiently for Him; do not fret when people succeed in their ways, when they carry out their wicked schemes.'

PSALM 37:3-7

Trust, delight, commit and be still. The harvest is coming.

Father,
Cause me to delight myself in you again. In the slowness of everything, I know that I have allowed myself to drop my expectancy and to let go of my faith a little. Change my enduring to delighting and change my cynicism to celebration as I reflect upon your word.
In Jesus' name, Amen.

I'M AWAKE!

> *'When Jacob awoke from his sleep, he thought, "Surely the*
> *Lord is in this place, and I was not aware of it." He was*
> *afraid and said, "How awesome is this place! This is none*
> *other than the house of God; this is the gate of Heaven."'*

GENESIS 28:16-17

In the same way that Jacob had to wake to see what God was doing around him, we need to wake up to realise that God is moving in our lives right now. Our unawareness of God and His ways needs to stop. Today, the God of Heaven is wanting to do something new in your life. God wants to advance you, He wants to grow your heart and He wants to fill your life with newness and freshness.

> *'Forget the former things; do not dwell on the past. See, I am doing*
> *a new thing! Now it springs up; do you not perceive it? I am*
> *making a way in the wilderness and streams in the wasteland.'*

ISAIAH 43:18-19

God declares that He's making all things new; new vessels, new ways of doing things, new strategies, new leadership and new places we have never been in before!

*'I will lead the blind by ways they have not known, along
unfamiliar paths I will guide them; I will turn the darkness into
light before them and make the rough places smooth.'*

ISAIAH 42:16

God doesn't want us to look at our today or our tomorrow with the filter of yesterday's experience.

You are the perfect candidate for a new thing. It's time to take off yesterday's filters of 'it's impossible', 'it has never happened before', 'I'm scared', 'I'm too old, I'm too young, I'm too weak, I'm too poor or I'm too sick to ever do it.'

*'The righteous will flourish like a palm tree, they will grow
like a cedar of Lebanon; planted in the house of the Lord,
they will flourish in the courts of our God. They will still
bear fruit in old age, they will stay fresh and green.'*

PSALM 92:12-14

Flourishing means growing luxuriously. It means increase and enlargement, blessing and abundance. Flourishing people stay fresh and green. They always sprout the green shoots of new ideas and thoughts.

Flourishing people live beyond themselves, they say no to containment or confinement, they choose to live in a large world and see the big picture. They pray for, live out and pursue 'God dreams.' And they are always busy producing, providing and pursuing many varied expressions of compassion to the world around them.

It's time to wake up, break out of containment and begin to flourish!

Father,
I choose to wake up to the new thing that you're doing in my world.
Help me to put off all excuses and do all I can to reposition myself to a
place where I can flourish for the Kingdom of God.
In Jesus' name, Amen.

DECLARATION SEVENTY-THREE

I HAVE A UNIQUE INHERITANCE

> '... I myself will drive them out before the Israelites. Be sure
> to allocate this land to Israel for an inheritance, as I have
> instructed you, and divide it as an inheritance among the
> nine tribes and half of the tribe of Manasseh.'
>
> **JOSHUA 13:6-7**

The clans of Israel were given many different types of territory to conquer. They were given different terrains, different land sizes and had to take on different conquests.

God has given each one of us different landscapes to possess, different inhabitants to minister to and different inheritances to get a hold of!

We tend to attempt to conquer our own landscapes with the same set of ministry tools as those in completely different neighbouring territories. There is a uniqueness to our calling—as individuals and as a church—that cannot be conquered with other people's tools.

Our commitment must be to never covet another person's inheritance or even another person's tools. To fight for the unique nature of what is meant to be yours is both your responsibility and your delight.

David complained when he was made to put on Saul's armour. He said, 'I cannot go in these ... because I am not used to them' (1 Samuel 17:39). He was called to use a sling, not a sword.

You have to be brave enough to embrace you. You then have to be brave enough to ignore the ridicule of those who don't believe in your uniqueness and your unique inheritance.

Today, it's time to ask yourself what you have taken on that is not really who you are. Where did you leave your own staff, shepherd's bag and sling? Did you leave it where it wasn't successful the first time? Did you leave it at the mercy of the opinion of a friend?

Church history is fashioned by those who pick up their inheritance, the mantle of their own unique anointing. And that's why you're here—to be pioneers of the shaping of God's church.

Father,

Thank you that, like the tribes of Israel, I have a unique territory to occupy. Thank you that I have been given the right 'equipment' to do this. Help me to resist simply copying someone else's methods to break into someone else's inheritance. I choose to love the land you've given me, to love the skin I'm in and love the abilities you've assigned to me to get the job done.

In Jesus' name, Amen.

DECLARATION SEVENTY-FOUR

I'M DRESSING FOR SUCCESS!

'Rather, clothe yourselves with the Lord Jesus Christ, and do not think about how to gratify the desires of the flesh.'
ROMANS 13:14

The Word of God places a big emphasis on clothing, but it's the clothing of the heart, not the body. It tells us what to put on and, sometimes more importantly, what we should take off. Let's take a look today at some clothing advice from the Word of God!

Firstly, don't wear your heart on your sleeve!

There is a certain composure that is needed that becomes helpful to everyone we meet. Learning to harness our emotions matures us as well as benefits others. Emotions are very deceptive things.

Many emotions are a rollercoaster you can't afford to ride. Emotional reliance is not beaten by logical thinking but by learning to know and trust God. If you bring emotion out to play without proper fences, it can greatly sabotage your future!

Secondly, don't get your knickers in a twist.

A lot of stupid things are said and done in anger! 'Fools give full vent to their rage, but the wise bring calm in the end' (Proverbs 29:11). The Bible says that the Lord is 'slow to anger.' Being 'Slow to anger' encourages understanding and strategy instead of inaccurate judgements and irreversible actions. Always put space between the upset and the response. Say to yourself regularly, "I will not react," and "I will wait and respond later".

Thirdly, don't be all dressed up and have nowhere to go.

It's time to be honest with the affairs of your heart. Often we can appear to be doing all the right things, yet when we go home we know deep down we are not being truly honest with who we are.

> 'Nothing in all creation is hidden from God's sight.
> Everything is uncovered and laid bare before the
> eyes of Him to whom we must give account.'
> **HEBREWS 4:13**

We can be all glammed up but with all of the wrong clothes—clothes that are too small for us (living a life hemmed by fear), too big for us (living somebody else's life), too last season for us (living in the old ways) and clothes that are just plain worn out (living in sheer exhaustion). You're dressed but there's no future destination for any of these outfits.

It's time to take a good look in the mirror and really think about your actions and attitudes. It's time to abandon pretence and embrace honesty—not honesty that abandons itself to emotions, but honesty that abandons itself to the Word of God.

Father,
Select clothing for me that's filled with authenticity, faith, kindness, love, self-control and patience. I now take all of my 'old clothes', bag them up and place them in the bin of redundancy. I don't need them or have any use for them anymore.
In Jesus' name, Amen.

DECLARATION SEVENTY-FIVE

I'M READY TO PLOUGH

'... *and break up your unploughed ground; for it is time to seek the Lord, until He comes and showers His righteousness on you.*'
HOSEA 10:12

When farmers want to grow crops on uncultivated soil, they need to go back to ploughing the field. It's only after ploughing that the ground is ready to bear a harvest. Unploughed grounds are the areas in our lives that are not fit to plant seed in—and because the ground can't take seed, it can never bear a harvest.

Today, we need to start ploughing the ground. The Bible tells us to:

'*Rend your heart and not your garments. Return to the Lord your God, for He is gracious and compassionate, slow to anger and abounding in love, and He relents from sending calamity.*'
JOEL 2:13

To rend is to tear up and break up. God asks us to rend our hearts, not our garments. Out of our hearts stem all the issues of life. Real 'rending' is laying out our hearts before God and saying, 'what do you need to change in me to bear fruit?' It is the attachment of our hearts to the heart of God.

And that takes digging up some of our over-attachments. Some of them are relational, some are to do with the past and some to do with an over-desire to succeed. Digging requires laying these things on the altar of sacrifice and purifying our worlds of all 'idols'. In doing so, our self-will is swallowed up in submission and our rebellion and defiance are halted by surrender to Christ.

After dealing with these 'roots', the weeds of attitude in our unploughed ground such as anger, sulkiness and jealousy can then be turned over and starved of the sunlight they need to keep on growing. Only then are we ready for planting.

> *'And afterward, I will pour out my Spirit on all people . . . and everyone who calls on the name of the Lord will be saved . . . '*
> ### JOEL 2:28-32

God promises provision, supernatural anointing and salvation after we attend to the rending of our hearts.

It's time to do some ploughing. For every new level of desiring God and His power, we need to do a new level of preparation. It's time to spend some time seeking God. We need to commit to be a people that does the mileage needed for the victory.

Father,
I'm ready to plough up my unploughed fields and get my heart and soul ready for a new season of fruitfulness and harvest. Thank you that from the same fields that created a hard heart, you are creating a soft heart ready to be seeded by your Word and your promise. I lay my heart before you now in deep and sincere submission.
In Jesus' name, Amen.

DECLARATION SEVENTY-SIX

THE HOLY SPIRIT EMPOWERS ME

*'The Israelites sampled their provisions
but did not inquire of the Lord.'*
JOSHUA 9:14

Have you ever had a really tough day and then had the realisation that you hadn't actually asked the Holy Spirit to help you at all?

Together with the Holy Spirit you are invincible. Yet, without Him you are powerless.

We often rush headlong into life, unaware that God the Holy Spirit wants to be intimately involved in all of the affairs and directions of our world. The Holy Spirit is our ever present help in all situations.

The Bible says if anyone lacks wisdom let him ask God. The Holy Spirit is living, active and working to speak into your life and direct your everyday. The Holy Spirit is alive, tender, loving, giving and guiding. He lives to fill you with the beauty of His presence.

'But you will receive power when the Holy Spirit comes on you . . . '
ACTS 1:8

We experience an empowerment when the Holy Spirit comes upon us. It's an empowerment to witness, an empowerment to prophesy, an empowerment to be envisioned and an empowerment to dream again.

*'But the Advocate, the Holy Spirit, whom the Father
will send in my name, will teach you all things and will
remind you of everything I have said to you.'*
JOHN 14:26

Today we need to realise that we cannot live any longer without the involvement and empowerment of the Holy Spirit.

If you need re-empowering and re-envisioning, we need to spend time today welcoming again the power and presence of the Holy Spirit.

If you have never been baptised in the Holy Spirit—today can be that very time. Ask Him to fill your 'inner you' with His Holy Spirit and God will do it. The Holy Spirit is ready to assist, ready to fill and ready to empower you to live a God-filled and God-directed life from this moment on.

Father,
I need your Spirit. Forgive me for rushing around in my own strength and for ignoring the promptings of the Spirit in my life. I want to connect now with that inner voice and be sensitively led by your wisdom and power. Fill me again and touch my heart. I'm ready to be led.
In Jesus' name, Amen.

DECLARATION SEVENTY-SEVEN

DESPERATION FUELS MY DARING

'... I will pour out my Spirit on all people. Your sons and daughters will prophesy, your young men will see visions, your old men will dream dreams. Even on my servants, both men and women, I will pour out my Spirit in those days, and they will prophesy.'

ACTS 2:17-18

God's intention is that we all live as people for whom connection with Heaven is normal—where dreams, visions, gifts of the Spirit, healing and miraculous power are all a normal part of our lives. It's time for our lives to reflect the true nature of a supernatural God. But how do we invite God's supernatural world into our world?

Firstly, we need to be desperate for more.

In Mark chapter 2, we read about Jesus healing a paralysed man. This guy was desperate for a miracle. He was desperate for a touch of Heaven to invade his world. There was no room left in the house so he didn't form a neat, orderly queue and he didn't come back another time. He got his friends to break through the roof on his behalf.

Don't just accept the natural state of affairs for your life. It is not OK. It is not OK to see the devil ripping people off, to see millions dying into a lost eternity, to see people suffering from broken hearts and broken minds, as well as seeing the injustice of people sold into sex slavery and labour gangs across our planet. Things are not OK. Let's be desperate about seeing our land healed.

> *'If my people, who are called by my name, will humble themselves and pray and seek my face and turn from their wicked ways, then will I hear from Heaven and forgive their sin and will heal their land.'*

2 CHRONICLES 7:14

Secondly, we need to be daring.

In John chapter 9, Jesus made mud with His saliva, wiped it on a man's eyes and told him to go and wash in the pool of Siloam. The man needed to be daring to get his miracle.

God requires many of us to be daring as well as desperate. There is always something to do in order to complete or initiate our miracles. Inaction paralyses our lives and paralyses our faith. It's time to be daring and to move into the realm of the Spirit we were born to reside in.

Father,
Lead me to that place. Make me hungry to see the supernatural become natural. Give me such a love for the broken that it drives me out from my own comforts and into an arena of pressing into you that causes mighty transfers of power to flow from Heaven.
In Jesus' name, Amen.

DECLARATION SEVENTY-EIGHT

MY CONFIDENCE IS IN GOD

'Do not throw away your confidence; it will be richly rewarded.'
HEBREWS 10:35

Confidence is a vital Kingdom commodity. Without it we lose the courage to get back onto the high seas of conquest and destiny. Confidence shows you have the right of possession.

The enemy's desire is to create divisions within our own spirit that strips us of our confidence.

'... Every Kingdom divided against itself will be ruined, and every city or household divided against itself will not stand.'
MATTHEW 12:25

Division often comes by questioning our capability to actually fulfil God's plan on the Earth. Somebody else is always better qualified.

Simon Peter was not a mighty leader when Jesus found him. He was a humble fisherman, yet God chose to build His church upon this man. Jesus told him the enemy would not overcome him, and promised him that He would give him all the keys of the Kingdom that he needed. He promised that whatever Simon Peter 'bound on earth would be bound in Heaven.'

God knows that we are but dust, but He still chooses to build His church upon us. He promises us that we will not be overcome by the enemy, and not be overcome by the sicknesses and strains of modern life. He promises us the keys of the Kingdom and all that we need, to do all that we need to do.

'Blessed are those whose strength is in you, whose hearts are set on pilgrimage. As they pass through the Valley of Baka, they make it a place of springs; the autumn rains also cover it with pools. They go from strength to strength, till each appears before God in Zion.'
PSALM 84:5-7

Good things happen to those who put their confidence in God.

Father,
I choose to line up the commitment of my mind with the convictions of my spirit. I choose to stop doubting and live by every word that proceeds out of the mouth of my God. Lift my confidence.
In Jesus' name, Amen.

DECLARATION SEVENTY-NINE

I AM BEING RENEWED

*'The angel of the Lord came back a second time and touched him
and said, "Get up and eat, for the journey is too much for you."'*
1 KINGS 19:7

Elijah had been busy doing what prophets do! He brought fire from
Heaven, came close to death and challenged the king in his pagan
worship. Elijah finally reached a place where he felt he could not go on.

You may have a picture of God as a hard taskmaster who doesn't
understand your mortality, but this passage shows us the truth. As we've
seen previously in this book, God has a beautiful understanding for
Elijah, and for humanity. Exhaustion is the place where your mortality
meets with the eternal. It's a foundation for the future.

*'Because He Himself suffered when He was tempted,
He is able to help those who are being tempted.'*
HEBREWS 2:18

We need to remember today that exhaustion is not the place to stop,
but the place to renew your strength. Your harvest lies on the other side
of God's waiting room of strength-replacement therapy.

*'Let us not become weary in doing good, for at the proper
time we will reap a harvest if we do not give up.'*
GALATIANS 6:9

We find ourselves trying many 'strength options' when our spirits are tired, whilst God's Word promises amazing strength from Heaven.

> *'But those who hope in the Lord will renew their strength.*
> *They will soar on wings like eagles; they will run and will*
> *not grow weary, they will walk and not be faint.'*
> **ISAIAH 40:31**

God's waiting room turns a place of fear and exhaustion into a place of anticipation and faith. God promises renewal, a birds-eye-view of God's perspective and the ability to keep on running towards the goal.

We're not meant, however, to stay waiting in the waiting room forever. There's a time where God will fill your tank and you'll be off again.

Father,
I'm here, waiting in your presence. Restore me, renew me, revive me and reinvent me. I thank you that you came to give me strength and that this is not the end but only an Ad break, a page between chapters and a short pause between seasons. Thank you for all of your promises. In Jesus' name, Amen.

DECLARATION EIGHTY

THE BATTLE IS WON IN THE TENT

'... but his young aide Joshua son of Nun did not leave the tent.'
EXODUS 33:11

We often gloss over this small tent that became Joshua's second home and focus on the day the walls of Jericho came tumbling down.

We read about this and then hear smatterings of what Joshua was up to through Exodus, Leviticus, Numbers and Deuteronomy until we reach the famous book of Joshua—when he rose up, won great victories and saw one of the greatest miracles in the entire Bible:

'The sun stopped in the middle of the sky and delayed going down about a full day. There has never been a day like it before or since, a day when the Lord listened to a human being...'
JOSHUA 10:13-14

This was the man who, when younger, never left the tent of the presence of God.

It's time to be found not just in church, but in seeking the God of the church! It's time to be hungry and desperate for an encounter with both God Himself and His power. We need to find and abide in the 'Tent of Personal Encounters.'

In Genesis 32, we read the story of Jacob wrestling with God. Once he recognized that he was wrestling with the Divine, he proclaimed, 'I won't let you go until you bless me!'

It was a full-on, determined wrestle, not a half-hearted play around with a couple of cushions. Like Jacob, do not leave, quit or give up until your hunger for God's power is satisfied.

It's very easy to become blasé and self-reliant whilst living in countries that are full of plenty. That's why our generosity should always take us back to 'the tent' of reliance.

We must realise that we can't represent God without soaking in His presence and receiving a touch of His power. Joshua also received a boldness in God's presence that became crucial in his quest to be a great leader of a nation. We read about it in Joshua chapter 1, when God continually told Joshua he needed to be 'strong and very courageous.'

You don't need self-help. You need a God-encounter—receive 'a different spirit' and become 'a different person.' Your commission doesn't happen on the main stage, it happens in the tent.

Joshua's biggest battles were won in the tent. And yours will be too.

Father,
Give me a hunger for an encounter with you. Help me to start to value your presence and to know that if my 'inner man' is filled and transformed, everything will be touched by it—my mind, my emotions, my relationships, my direction and my future world.
In Jesus' name, Amen.

DECLARATION EIGHTY-ONE

I CHOOSE TO CLIMB

'In their hearts humans plan their course,
but the Lord establishes their steps.'
PROVERBS 16:9

What happens when you plan a course of action only to find that your planning goes completely awry?

Do we look for people to blame?

Do we curse it as demonic?

Do we have a toddler tantrum?

Do we blame ourselves?

Or do we think that maybe the hand of the Lord might actually be in the midst of it?

It seems like just as we plan a nice easy route for our lives to take, a mountain appears in our way. Yet this is what the Word of God says about mountains:

'... On the mountain of the Lord it will be provided.'
GENESIS 22:14

Today could be your day to commit to the climb: to allow God to encourage you to not bail out mid-mountain and to allow God to strengthen your capacity and build inner strength. So many of God's promises rest upon us committing to the climb!

It is always a mid-mountain experience that tempts us to quickly get off the mountain and abort the climb. Familiarity wants to take us back to a life of predictability even if it had lost its joy and its freshness. There is, however, real joy in just one glimpse of the supernatural hand of God. There's real excitement as we contemplate Heaven's breakthrough upon us, as we imagine our lives on the other side of the mountain filled with the colours of Heaven. The climb is redeemed by the touch of His hand upon us.

The end of the climb is always astonishing:

> *'Instead of bronze, I will bring you gold, and silver*
> *in place of iron. Instead of wood I will bring you*
> *bronze, and iron in place of stones.'*
> **ISAIAH 60:17**

God promises unnatural promotions, supernatural advancement, and ever-increasing transfers from Heaven that supersede the natural order of things. He promises multiplication instead of addition and a complete change in the economy of our worlds.

God's encouragement to us today is to get back on the climb and to drop the abseiling rope that tempts us to abort the next section of our journey.

We know deep inside that our climb will not only lead to God's amazing blessings, but will also inspire a generation.

Father,
I'm in! Your ways often involve mountains being conquered, not by their removal but by the climb. I know that you will get me onto the other side. Help me not to stop, not to fight it and not to complain about it. Fill me with the joy of your presence and an expectation of breakthrough. In Jesus' name, Amen.

DECLARATION EIGHTY-TWO

SLOW DOES NOT MEAN NO

*'After sending them home, He went up into
the hills by Himself to pray ...'*
MATTHEW 14:23

Jesus was never driven by the crowds. He often went the second mile in His love for people, but He was never driven by a need to please or a need to conform. In Matthew chapters 14 and 15, Jesus withdrew from the crowd four times in order to recoup, pray and get refilled for the journey ahead.

Even with the needs of the people pressing in on Him, He still withdrew and slowed down the pace of His life.

There is a 'sacred slowing down' that's waiting for you too. If your phone freezes, the usual way to get it working again is to switch it off for a while and then switch it back on. And it's the same with you.

Rest and recalibration are part of a successful life. And reconnecting to the source of life and power is a sure key for greater breakthrough, not less.

In a world of the fast and the furious, the 'sacred slow' of the Kingdom of God reigns. Slow is the new perfect.

*'But do not forget this one thing, dear friends: with the Lord a
day is like a thousand years, and a thousand years are like a day.
The Lord is not slow in keeping His promise, as some understand*

slowness. Instead He is patient with you, not wanting anyone to perish, but everyone to come to repentance.'
2 PETER 3:8-9

To say that a day is like a thousand years would give the impression that God has no idea of timing, yet what it actually indicates is that God is not driven by timing. Because He knows the end from the beginning, He knows there's no need to hustle and rush. God might seem slow, but slow and certain is better than fast and furious. Slow and steady beats fast and erratic, every time.

Slow does not mean no. His timing is perfect. His ways are just . . . right. Let's get back to the 'unforced rhythm of grace' as He leads us to green pastures and still waters.

Father,
Still my heart and let me know again that you are God. Give me a peace deep within and a sense of 'sabbath rest' so that everything I do comes out from that place and not from a place of fear and doubt. Calm me down and give me the wisdom to know that time out does not mean time up and slow does not mean no.
In Jesus' name, Amen.

DECLARATION EIGHTY-THREE

I CARE ABOUT MY SHADOW

'As a result, people brought the sick into the streets and laid them on beds and mats so that at least Peter's shadow might fall on some of them as he passed by.'

ACTS 5:15

Everywhere you go, you cast a shadow onto the world around you. It's everything you are when you're not paying attention to who you are. It's the person you're becoming when you're not in the spotlight of public attention. It's the 'other you.'

They say that when someone preaches, what creates the biggest impact isn't the words of the person but their persona. It's not found so much in their stories or in their ability to connect; it's found in their stature, their afterthoughts and their glint—what they say between the lines, not in the lines.

It's your shadow. The residue that you leave can work for good, or work for bad. For Peter, he left a sense of the presence and power of God, like an aroma that lingered in the air, and it had the power to heal!

Addressing your shadow can unlock a secret doorway to ministry. The little things you do can leave a bigger impact and impression than any of the bigger things that you do and say whilst in the public eye; the small words of encouragement you give, the prayers that you pray and the sincere love that you have for the most fragile.

Let's attend to our shadows and change our world for the better.

This is what Paul says about 'Shadow Ministry' -

*'Therefore, as God's chosen people, holy and dearly loved, clothe
yourselves with compassion, kindness, humility, gentleness and
patience. Bear with each other and forgive one another if any of
you has a grievance against someone. Forgive as the Lord forgave
you. And over all these virtues put on love, which binds them
all together in perfect unity. Let the peace of Christ rule in your
hearts, since as members of one body you were called to peace.
And be thankful. Let the message of Christ dwell among you
richly as you teach and admonish one another with all wisdom
through psalms, hymns, and songs from the Spirit, singing
to God with gratitude in your hearts. And whatever you do,
whether in word or deed, do it all in the name of the Lord Jesus,
giving thanks to God the Father through Him.'*
COLOSSIANS 3:12-17

Look after your shadow and your shadow will look after you.

*Father,
I realise that my impact comes both from the public me and the private
me. Help me to look after my shadow so that it heals many, releases
many and frees many as I live with and walk by the lives of others.
In Jesus' name, Amen.*

DECLARATION EIGHTY-FOUR

I CAN ALWAYS BOUNCE BACK

'The Lord said to Samuel, "How long will you mourn
for Saul, since I have rejected him as king over Israel?
Fill your horn with oil and be on your way."'
1 SAMUEL 16:1

Sometimes the pathway to God's fulfilment over our lives has many twists and turns. We need to bounce back well and learn to negotiate the journey with both faith and trust.

It's easy when we have knockbacks and setbacks to question whether we are still in the middle of the will of God or not. Samuel knew that the kingship of Saul was coming to an end. God told him to stop crying and go and anoint the next king—the next move of God.

I love the moment where David was actually chosen by God to be the next king. God spoke to Samuel and said, 'The Lord does not look at the things man looks at. Man looks at the outward appearance, but the Lord looks at the heart' (1 Samuel 16:7).

Your future is not determined by how impressive your resume is or isn't. It's determined by the softness and obedience of your heart.

Somebody will always look more impressive than you, but that does not deny that you have been chosen by God.

'There is still the youngest, but he is tending the sheep.'
1 SAMUEL 16:11

God knows your address and sees your faithfulness. It's a secret the devil doesn't want you to know about. King David faced opposition when he spoke out his desire to face Goliath. His big brother belittled him and then said "I know how conceited you are". Even King Saul chipped in with, 'You are only a boy and he's been a man of war since his youth!' David was well and truly downsized by all.

David's response to the king was magnificent. 'Your servant has killed both the lion and the bear.' (1 Samuel 17:36)

Don't allow criticism to stop you entering destiny. Don't allow criticism to rob you of what you do best!

> *Father,*
> *Today I prophesy over my future, even in the midst of the battle I find myself in. I prophesy success over the spirit of denial and disappointment. I prophesy success over the spirit of accusation and judgement. I prophesy over that which seems either totally impossible or totally dead in my world. I prophesy the breath of Heaven onto the battlefield and proclaim that victory is mine.*
> *In Jesus' name, Amen.*

ABOUT THE AUTHOR

Jenny Gilpin was the founder of City Hearts, a UK charity that cared for over 3,500 clients with a team of 170 people, an organisation that eventually multiplied its reach through partnerships in Ghana and the Netherlands. Their work also helped shape victim care legislation in the UK.

Jenny's heart for people is founded within her incredible story of healing and hope. At three weeks old, she was adopted by a family that took her as their own, lavishing her with care and every opportunity, but she struggled with rejection and perfectionism. The unknowns of her past and her shrouded identity drove her to seek out her biological mother in an attempt to find herself. It was only at sixteen, through a profound encounter with God that Jenny experienced the breakthrough her heart desired. What she found in her new relationship with the Holy Spirit ignited a passion in her to help other people.

Jenny and her husband Dave, founded and established churches in Britain before moving to the Gold Coast, Australia. They are now itinerant ministers and Jenny is also a not-for-profit coach.

Follow Jenny on Instagram
@jennygilpin